AFRICAN EMPIRES

—— VOLUME 1 ——

YOUR GUIDE TO THE
HISTORICAL RECORD OF AFRICA

J.P. MARTIN

Trafford rev. 10/21/2017

 www.trafford.com

North America & international
toll-free: 1 888 232 4444 (USA & Canada)
fax: 812 355 4082

ACKNOWLEDGEMENTS

This book is dedicated to my creator, my mother, father, grandmothers, sister, the special lady in my life, and friends who have provided consistent love and support throughout this project.

CONTENTS

INTRODUCTION

The continent of Africa is home to the first human civilizations on planet earth. It is understood to be the oldest inhabited territory on Earth. Africa is 11.7 million square miles making it the 2nd largest continent on earth and Africa covers 20.4 percent of the total land area on earth. The earliest human beings on planet earth can be traced back to Africa living in around 250,000 BC. For example, the remains of African people have been found in East Africa, within the area of Ethiopia called the Omo Kibish Formation which date back to 130,000 BC. Africa is also the region in which the human race first developed language, writing, science, mathematics, architecture, agriculture, religion and military strategy. The continent of Africa is the location where the world's first kingdoms and empires were created. The historical record of humankind begins in Africa and therefore it is important for us to understand the magnificent history of these great ancient African empires, kingdoms and their cultures.

The subject of African history is one which needs to be explored in detail if we are to understand the foundation of all of the human civilizations and human achievements on planet earth. African history unfortunately has often been a neglected subject which this research project seeks to help rectify. Through detailed analysis and new archaeological research methods we are now finally beginning to understand the true history of Africa and its vital contribution to mankind as the creator and developer of the majority of human social systems and scientific developments that we take for granted in our modern age. The history of Africa and its empires is an enormous, colourful and fascinating subject. The rich history of this magnificent region is a story which must be understood, respected and taught, it is a story of mighty kings and queens, conquest and glory.

When we look at African history we soon discover that there were major empires and civilizations across every region of the African continent.

Across all of Africa large cities were established and a rich and diverse culture was present as well as numerous royal dynasties which span hundreds and in some cases thousands of years. In North Africa we find significant trade routes being established, numerous successful military expeditions being conducted. We have some of the earliest human beings being found in East Africa and the development of sophisticated mathematics, astronomy and science. In West Africa we find some of the largest empires covering territories of enormous size and a rich culture of scholarship and book production. Across South Africa we find sophisticated stone construction taking place and trade being organised between Africa and Asia.

The African Empires Research Project has been conducted over a number of years through intensive study and detailed research utilizing respected sources and recent archeological studies. The African Empires Research Project has now produced a number of resources and books on the topic of African history. The African Empires book series has been produced in a series of volumes which provide a detailed record on the major African empires and kingdoms across thousands of years. Each chapter within the volumes will focus on a specific African civilization and present their major achievements, culture and historical record.

Overview of African Empires Volume 1

In African Empires Volume 1 we looked at the following empires across a series of chapters.
Chapter 1: Early Civilization in Africa
Chapter 2: Archaeological Sites of Early Africa
Chapter 3: Ancient Pre-Dynastic Cultures in North-East Africa
Chapter 4: The Naqada Kingdoms
Chapter 5: The Nubian Empire: Part 1
Chapter 6: The Kingdom of Kush
Chapter 7: The Nubian Empire: Part 2
Chapter 8: Ancient Egypt
Chapter 9: The Kingdom of Ethiopia
Chapter 10: The Empire of Ghana
Chapter 11: The Empire of Mali
Chapter 12: Historical Timeline of Africa
Chapter 13: Conclusion

Overview of African Empires Volume 2

In African Empires Volume 2 we looked at the following empires across a series of chapters.
Chapter 1: Archaeological Sites of Early Africa: Part 2
Chapter 2: The Songhai Empire
Chapter 3: The Nok Kingdom
Chapter 4: The Kingdom of Carthage
Chapter 5: The Almoravid Dynasty
Chapter 6: The Almohad Dynasty
Chapter 7: The Kanem Empire
Chapter 8: The Benin Empire
Chapter 9: The Hausa Kingdoms
Chapter 10: Great Zimbabwe
Chapter 11: The Swahili Kingdoms
Chapter 12: Historical Timeline of Africa
Chapter 13: Conclusion

CHAPTER 1

Early Civilization in Africa

The first human beings on planet earth developed in Africa in around 250,000 BC. Sometimes known as the 'Recent African Origin Model' or RAO for short, it is understood by historians and scientists across the world that all human life started in the continent of Africa and then spread out slowly to other regions across the earth over a period of thousands of years starting in around 125,000 BC. This scientific theory is also known as the Out of Africa (OOA) hypothesis. In 2003, the oldest human remains on earth were discovered in Herto, Ethiopia which is located in east Africa. These human remains have been dated by scientists to be approximately 160,000 years old. In 1967 a group of bones found at the Omo Kibish Formation, near the Ethiopian Kibish Mountains were found and these are believed to be 130,000 years old.

The Geographical Landscape of Africa

The continent of Africa is the 2nd largest continent on planet earth and is surrounded by a number of sea's and oceans. To the north of Africa, the Mediterranean Sea separates the continent of Europe from Africa. To the north east the Red Sea is located which separates Africa from modern-day Saudi Arabia and the Middle-East. To the east of Africa, the Indian Ocean is located and to the west of Africa the Atlantic Ocean is located. The equator, which is an imaginary line used by geographers which circles the earth and is equidistant between the north and south poles runs through the centre of Africa. Africa has always been home to various types landscapes including forests, jungles, deserts, mountains, hills, water basins, rivers and coastal areas with beaches. There are some well-known geographical areas of Africa including the Atlas Mountains, which are a grouping of mountains in northern Africa which extends from modern-day Morocco in the north-east through Algeria to Tunisia.

The total length of the Atlas Mountains is 1600 miles (2500 kilometres) and the tallest mountain is 13,671 feet (4167 metres) in height. Another well-known geographical area is the Nile River which is positioned in north-eastern Africa and is the longest river on planet earth. The Nile River runs from modern-day Egypt to Sudan and also flows into Ethiopian, Eritrea, Tanzania, Uganda, Rwanda, Burundi, Congo and Kenya.

The Namib Desert is the oldest desert on planet earth and is located in south-western Africa and stretches along the coast of modern-day Angola, Namibia and South Africa. The total length of The Namib Desert is 1200 miles (2000 kilometres). The Congo Basin in Central Africa is the 2nd largest river basin on planet earth (a river basin is an area of land drained by a river and its branches). The Congo Basin is 1.3 million square miles in size (3.4 million kilometres). The Congo Basin consists of dense forests, rivers and swamps and is home to over 10,000 species of tropical plants. The Sahara Desert which used to be covered in vegetation and lakes is now the largest desert on planet earth covering a distance of 3,600,000 square miles (9,400,000 square kilometres). Mosi-oa-Tunya (also known as Victoria Falls) is the largest waterfall in African and located on the Zambezi River on the border of modern-day Zimbabwe and Zambia. Lou (also known as Lake Victoria) is the 2nd largest fresh water lake in the world and located on the border of modern-day Tanzania, Uganda and Kenya. The continent of Africa is home to over 1100 species of mammals, 2600 species of birds and 20,000 species of plant life. Africa is also home to the largest land animal on planet earth the African Elephant, the tallest animal the African Giraffe and the fastest land animal the African Cheetah.

Human Origins in Africa

Historians, scientists, anthropologist and archaeologists around the world are now in complete and unanimous agreement that the human race of planet earth originated in Africa. Africans were first established on earth in around 250,000 BC. Around 50,000 BC the African who were the only human beings existing on planet earth at that time began to move out of Africa into Australasia, Arabia, Asia and Europe. In the present day we can find examples of peoples in regions outside Africa who look very similar to Africans. Amongst the original inhabitants of Australia of the present-day we find the Aboriginal Australians who still retain the features of their African ancestors. Also in Melanesia, which includes Papua New Guinea, Fiji, Solomon Islands and Vanuatu again we find the original inhabitants retaining the features of their African ancestors. The same examples can be found amongst the original inhabitants of the Polynesian islands. In addition, indigenous peoples of Malaysia called the 'Semang' tribe, the indigenous peoples of Thailand called the 'Maniq' tribe and the indigenous people of the Philippines called Agta are virtually indistinguishable from native Africans. Research conducted by Oxford University in England, UK and Stanford in California, USA has found that Melanesians from New Guinea and Aborigines from Australia share much of the same genetics as their African ancestors and are linked to the original expansion of Africans out of the continent and into other regions of the planet in 50,000 BC.

Early on the earth was one land mass, the Africans used a number of pathways to populate the earth, which included moving north-east from Ethiopia to Yemen and into Arabia and then into western Asia and then into eastern Asia with some settling in the modern-day region of Russia. Other Africans continued on into far eastern Asia and into the North American region and then central and southern America. Another route the Africans took was from Africa, through Arabia and into eastern and then western Europe. Finally, the African also moved out of Africa into Arabia and then West and Eastern Asia and down into South-East Asian and Australia, Polynesia and Melanesia. Skin colour variations amongst the human beings from dark to light came about due to the quantity of Melanin in the skin depending on the region of the planet humans were living in. Melanin is the main determinant of skin colour and eye colour. Melanin also aids humans in human reproduction because protects against folate depletion which is required for organ development. Melanin also protects the skin from damage and reduces signs of aging. There is also another type of Melanin known as Neuromelanin which is present within the brain in larger quantities in humans and much lesser in other species such as animals. Melanin also protects humans from ultra-violet radiation and skin-cancer. Human beings with higher exposure to the sun such as the African retained their melanin and darker skin complexions while humans with lower exposure to sun such as those who remained in Europe eventually lost their Melanin

Africa and Human Genetics

In the field of human genetics, the name "Mitochondrial Eve" refers to the most recent common ancestor in a direct, unbroken, maternal line, of all currently living humans for females. The name Mitochondrial Eve is a reference to the first human female mentioned in the Bible created by God who is named Eve. Similarly, the term "Y-chromosomal Adam" refers to the most recent common ancestor in a direct, unbroken, maternal line, of all currently living humans for males. The name Y-chromosomal Adam is a reference to the first human male mentioned in the Bible created by God who is named Adam. Both Mitochondrial Eve and Y-chromosomal Adam are believed to have lived in Eastern Africa over 250,000 years ago by modern geneticists. DNA is a molecule that encodes the genetic instructions used in the development and functioning of all living organisms. In 1987, a group of geneticists published a study that examined the DNA taken from 147 people across all current modern day racial groups. The geneticists found that the lineage of all people alive today falls on one of two branches in the human family tree. One of these branches consists of nothing but African lineage, the other contains all other groups, including some African lineage.

The Bantu Expansion

The Bantu were and are an African people which encapsulate over 500 different ethnic groups which all speak one or more of the 500 Bantu languages inclusive of Zulu, Shona and Swahili. Originating in Western

Africa (eastern Cameroon and western Nigeria) the Bantu people expanded in 2000 BC across a huge territory eventually encompassing the entire region of Sub-Saharan Africa (the territory below the Sahara Desert) previously populated by the Khoisan peoples. The Khoisan People are an African group who were located in modern-day Angola, Namibia, Botswana and South Africa. The Khoisan are divided into the San people and the Khoikhoi people. The Bantu Expansion itself describes the migration out of West Africa and their movement into Central and Southern Africa with a smaller group entering into East Africa. By 1000 BC the Bantu people had located themselves in the Great Lakes region of Eastern Africa.

The Great Lakes region consists of 15 of the largest fresh water lakes on planet earth which include Nyanza (also known as Lake Victoria). The mass migration lasted 2000 years by which point the Bantu people had reached modern-day Zimbabwe and South Africa. The Bantu people eventually went on to establish numerous powerful African kingdoms inclusive of the Mutapa Empire and Great Zimbabwe in Southern Africa. The reason that the Bantu migrated across Africa from their original location are thought to be because the rulers wanted to expand the territory and establish new empires, the fertile grasslands of the Sahara began to dry up, the Bantu wanted to utilize the iron working that they had perfected in Western Africa for use in agricultural development in new areas. The Bantu expansion had many benefits for the continent as technological developments in iron-smelting and iron-working were spread around the entire continent. Food production increased and hunting was now supported with agricultural development and land cultivation across Africa.

Language Development in Africa

Africans were the first human beings to develop spoken language. African languages across the continent have been traced to have four common regions. Firstly, the Nilo Saharan language family developed in eastern Africa between the Nubian mountains and the middle of the

5

Nile River. This language family spread west close to the Lake Chad area underneath the Sahara region which at this time was green and fertile. Secondly, the Niger-Congo language family orginated in central Africa region near the Congo Forest and was utilized somewhat by the Lupemban culture of that area. The people of the Lupemban culture are thought to have lived around 30,000 BC. This language family eventually spread into West Africa.

Thirdly, the Khosian language family has its origins in eastern Africa, in the area that is modern day Tanzania. This language family spread out into southern Africa. It is also from this family that the Sandawe language spoken in modern day Tanzania is thought to have arisen. Lastly, the Afro-Asiatic language developed in eastern Africa in the area between Northern Sudan and the Ethiopian highlands. This language family spread out into the areas around Northern Kenya and Somalia. The development of language across Africa allowed knowlegde to be communicated and early technical developments to spread more quickly adding to the rich cultures that began to emerge at this time.

Development of African Mathematics

The Africans were the first peoples on earth to develop mathematics and counting tools which formed the basis for modern day advanced mathematics. Some of the most notable artifacts for calculation include the Lebombo Bone (Swaziland), Ishango Bone (Zaire/Congo), Moscow Papyrus (Egypt), Rhind Papyrus (Egypt), Timbuktu Manuscripts (Mali) and the Mancala Game (Ethiopia).

The Lebombo Bone

The Lebombo Bone was discovered in the Lebombo Mountains which are located in Southern Africa near modern day Swaziland. The bone is from a baboon skeleton and has been dated to back to 43,000 BC. Located on the bone are 29 notches used for mathematical calculations by early Arrficans and is the oldest mathematical instrument in the world. Historians understand that the bone was used to track the lunar cycles and phases which reference the revolution of the earth around the sun.

Ishango Bone

The Ishando Bone was discovered in the area of Ishango near the Semliki River in north eastern Congo loacted in Central Africa. The bone is from the skeleton of a baboon and has been dated back to 20,000 BC. Located on the bone are three columns of notches grouped together. The numbers on both the right and left columns are all odd numbers which are 9,11, 13, 17, 19, 21 and it is understood that the bone was used as a counting tool for mathematical equations. It is also understood that this bone may have been used to track lunar cycles.

Egyptian Mathematical Leather Roll

The Egyptian Mathematical Leather Roll was discovered in the North-East Africa in Egypt and dates back to 1650 BC and is thought to have been developed during the 16th Dynasty of Egypt. The Egyptian Mathematical Leather Roll is also known by its abbreviated form EMLR. The size of the scroll is approximately 25 centimtres long (10 inches) and 43 centimetres wide (17 inches). The scroll was unrolled in 1927 AD and provides a listing of 26 mathematical fractions and are divided in two columns, these fractions teach African mathematical theory. The formulars aided the Egyptians in caluclating and mesuring. The EMLR was found along with the Egyptian Mathematical Papyrus.

Egyptian Mathematical Leather Papyrus

The Egyptian Mathematical Papyrus is an ancient Egyptian mathematical papyrus artifact and dates back to 1650 BC. The Egyptian

Mathematical Leather Papyrus is also known as the Rhind Mathematical Papyrus or RMP. The Egyptian Mathematical Leather Papyrus contains 85 mathematical execerceis and a table of fractions. The introdcution to the papyrus written by the Egyptians reads 'Accurate reckoning for inquiring into things, and the knowledge of all things, mysteries and secrets'.

Early Art and Agricultural Development in Africa

The first human artwork on earth was discovered in the Blombos Cave which is located in South Africa approximately 300 kilometers east of Cape Town. Archeologists excavating the site have found carving tools created by the early Africans that lived there made from Quartzite which is a type of rock. In addition, other artefacts found include materials used for painting. Containers made from shells as well as red and yellow colors painted on the walls of the cave were found and these indicate a relatively advanced method of producing the artwork located inside the caves. The age of the contents of this cave are thought by archeologists to be around 70,000 years old. In 11,000 BC in west Africa in modern day Nigeria in the area known as Akure numerous rock paintings were also developed. The development of crop cultivation in early Africa was an important component to the gradual expansion of control over the natural environment.

Cultivation of plants and crops began when the early Africans began to deliberately sow seeds, remove weeds and look after large sections of vegetaion for the purpose of organizing a consistent food supply. In a similar fashion certain animals would be herded, protected and fed by these early Africans for the production of milk and eventually meat. By controlling the plantlife and animals around them the Africans were able to gradually develop larger permanent communities and this resulted in an increase in the African population as birth rates increased. Members of these early communities would work in the fields from an early age ensuring a constant food supply for the whole group and becoming the first farmers. In addition permanent housing was developed and also pottery was designed and produced. In 2007 AD a Swiss archaeologist from Geneva University discovered pieces of pottery in western Africa in Mali in an area called the Bandiagara Cliffs which are thought to have been created in 9,500 BC.

The pottery discovered in Mali is some of the oldest in Africa. Another early African group that also developed pottery and clay artifacts were the Badarian culture. The Badarian culture of pre-dynastic Egypt developed around 5,000 BC and lived in small villages in the area of Upper Egypt and Northern Nubia. This group also developed agriculture. Archeologists that have conducted extensive digging within this region have found over 600 graves. Badarian pottery consisted of reddish-brown vessels with black-tipped rims. Pottery was mass produced by a community of craftsmen. The Africans located in the north east of Africa domesticated cattle around the year 3500 BC and the territory they controlled encompassed modern-day Eritrea, Somalia and Northern Kenya. They also spread to northern Tanzania between 3500 BC and 1000 BC. The Africans located within the Sahara during the period beginning in 4000 BC were heavily engaged in the raising of livestock and were skilled in the care and raising of animals. The area they inhabited covered the Ahagga Mountains towards the east of the Sahara and the Tibesti mountains to the east. The paintings they left behind depicted large herds of cattle and sheep.

The Africans of the Sahara also cultivated millet and beans. Farming in West Africa had begun even earlier and since 9000 BC they had been developing agricultural practices cultivating yams and groundnuts and the kola nut. The territory that these Africans controlled encompassed Niger and part of the Congo. By 3000 BC the Africans that lived within this region had begun the domestication of rice and this practice spread further west wards and reached Guinea and Liberia. A notable group known as the Nok kingdom were established at around 1000 BC and controlled the region of Northern Nigeria in West Africa. The Nok kingdom are well known for producing many art works and continued to do so until around 300 AD. The Nok are well known for utilizing clay to create very detailed artifacts and producing terracotta sculptures of heads, animals, figures and pottery. Eyes of a triangular shape are typical of their style. Other artifacts of the Nok culture include iron tools, stone axes stone tools and stone ornaments.

Astronomy in Early Africa

Astronomy is the scientific study of the cosmos which includes the analysis of star systems, planets, moons and galaxies. In Africa the study of astronomy dates back to 4800 BC and was conducted by African kingdoms across the continent at different times. The African utilized scientific instruments and documented their usage. Some of the African kingdoms and nations which were heavily involved in astronomy included the following:

Astronomy in West Africa: The Dogon

The Dogon people are an African group which are from West Africa and in the region of modern-day Mali south of the Niger River. The Dogon established themselves in the area in about prior to 1000 AD. The Dogon were masters of astronomy and studied the stars and planets in-depth. The Dogon believe in one God called 'Amma' or 'Amen' who they believe to be the creator and originator of the universe and planet earth including all of creation, they are monotheists in this regard. The Dogon cosmology and sacred knowledge was held by their priests which are organized into an order which require initiation. The Dogon are famous around the world amongst scientists for the astronomical knowledge they had prior to the invention of telescopes. They were aware of the star fifty-year orbital period of the star Sirius, the Dogon also had knowledge of the moons surrounding Jupiter and the rings of Saturn. It is still not fully understood how these African were able to obtain such detailed knowledge without the aid of modern technology.

Astronomy in West Africa: The Serer

The Serer people are a West African group from the region of modern-day Senegal near to the Gambian Border. The Serer established themselves in the region prior to 1000 AD. The Serer people studied the star systems and developed their own cosmology. The Serer people believe in one God which they called 'Roog' and that is who they consider to be the supreme creator of the entire universe. Roog is also known as 'Roog Dangandeer Seen' which translates into English as 'the omnipresent God'. They were are monotheistic people. The word the Serer use for the creation of the universe is 'A nax' and they have a detailed creation story and religion. The Serer possessed knowledge of the axis of the world and the positioning of the planets and also depicted the rotation of the earth. Like the Dogon they considered Sirius to be an important Star system. The Serer developed diagrams of the universe and star systems and the relationship between Roog and the creation. The Serer also later developed the Kingdom of Sine in West Africa prior to 1300 AD.

Astronomy in East African: Ancient Nubia

The Nubians are an African group which established themselves in East Africa in the area of modern-day Sudan in around 4800 BC. The Nubians studied the stars and developed detailed astronomical knowledge which they documented in monument and artifacts. The Nubians tracked the procession of the stars and their movements. One of the more well know astronomical monuments is The Nabta Playa which is also known as the world's oldest astronomical observatory. The Nabta Playa is located near Nabta in the Nubian desert in East Africa. The Nabta Playa consists of a series of stone circles, stone slabs, buried rocks with carvings and megalithic structures. The stone structures are astronomically aligned to the stars, including the seven-star constellation known as the 'big dipper', the Orion constellation and the star Sirius.

Astronomy in East Africa: Ancient Kenya

In East Africa the Turkana ethnic group are an African people located to the south of the Nile River near South-Sudan in the Turkana Region of modern-day Kenya. Namoratunga which was developed by the Turkana in 300 BC is an astronomical site located on the west side of Lake Turkana in eastern Kenya on the border of Sudan and Ethiopia. At Namoratunga, stone structures were constructed by the Turkana including 19 pillars. The Turkana studied the movement of the stars and aligned their stone structures to 7 key star systems including Sirius, Orion, Saiph, Aldebaran, Bellatrix, Pleiades and Triangulum. The astronomical site was used to track the 354-day lunar calendar which the Turkana follows.

Astronomy in North East Africa: Ancient Egypt

In North-East Africa the Egyptian civilization located near to the Nile River also were keen observers of the stars. The Egyptians documented their knowledge of the stars in what historians have termed 'diagonal star tables'. The Egyptians used these star tables to track time. A typical star table consisted of 40 columns with each column representing a 10-day period. Each column was aligned to a particular star. The Egyptian called the star Sirius 'the sharp one' and the star constellation of Orion was also of importance. The Egyptian were also aware of the planets such as Mars, Saturn, Jupiter, Mercury and Venus. The Egyptian star tables date back to 2000 BC.

Trade in Early Africa

With the continent of Africa being so large the early Africans had to develop trade routes between the numerous empires and kingdoms for the exchange of goods and services. In terms of size from a geographical perspective Africa is larger than China, India and Europe combined. Some of the trade routes and connections included the following:

The Trade Between the Empire of Nubia and Ancient Egypt

The Nubian Empire (located in modern-day Sudan) and the Egyptian Empire (located in modern-day Egypt) because of their close geographical proximity and common ancestry engaged in frequent trade. Both civilizations utilized donkeys and later camels to carry goods between the two nations over the roads which they developed. We find on the tomb Harkhuf of the governor of southern Egypt the following inscription of the goods his people obtained from Nubia:

"We had 300 donkeys laden with incense, ebony, oil, aromatics, panther skins, ivory carvings, boomerangs and other good products".

Nubia itself mined gold and cultivated ivory in vast quantities which they traded with Egypt to the north. Egypt cultivated and sold to Nubia grain, linen, oils and also salt and papyrus, the latter of which was used for writing.

The Trade Between the Ghana Empire and Kingdom of Morocco

The Empire of Ghana located in western Africa at the height of their power controlled the gold and salt trade in the region. Ghana was known as the 'Land of Gold'. The Empire of Ghana worked alongside the Wangara who were a West African Islamic group well established in the gold trade by 800 AD. The Wangara were known for their gold mining skills and Islamic scholarship. Within the region gold fields were later located to the south in Bambuk and Bure. The territory which the Wangara controlled was a great commercial center in western Africa at the time. The Ghana Empire was the most powerful state in western Africa and in this period controlled a large area of territory. The Wangara would mine the gold keeping the specific locations of mines secret and by collaborating with the Empire of Ghana both parties had virtually full control over the gold market.

The Empire of Ghana established trade agreements with the African Berbers who were situated in North Africa which included the Kingdom of Morocco. The Kingdom of Morocco at this time was Islamic and controlled by the African Berbers who had established the city of Sijilmasa in south-eastern Morocco under the leadership of the Idrisid Dynasty. The Ghana Empire from their capital Koumbi Saleh which was the largest city in western Africa administrated the trade of gold, salt and kola nuts. The Ghana Empire imported bars of salt and cloth from the Kingdom of Morocco in the north of Africa and exchanged it for gold and kola nuts which they harvested from western Africa. From North Africa gold would reach Europe, the Middle-East and Asia.

The Trade Between the Kingdom of Zimbabwe and The Swahili Kingdoms

By 700 AD the Swahili people had established the Swahili Kingdoms in eastern Africa from Mogadishu (modern-day Somalia) southward down to Sofala (modern-day Mozambique). By 1000 AD The Swahili Kingdoms were the most powerful group in the region and controlled the fishing trade off the eastern coast of Africa. Their close proximity to Arabia allowed them to establish trade with the foreign Arab nations. These links allowed the Africans to get their products as far as Persia and India. The Swahili people were great sailors and built many merchant ships which they used for trade. By 1075 AD the Shona people in southern Africa had established the Kingdom of Zimbabwe and constructed their central city named Great Zimbabwe (modern-day Zimbabwe). The Kingdom of Zimbabwe was to the west of the Swahili Kingdoms. The two kingdoms began to establish trade links soon after each kingdom consolidated their power as unified nation. Great Zimbabwe produced goods such as gold, ivory, iron, timber, animal skins, frankincense, grain, and salt. A key trading city for the Swahili Kingdom was Kilwa. At Kilwa, the Swahili people imported goods from China such as porcelain, and jewellery from India. Import and export taxes were put on top of good flowing in and out of the

Swahili Kingdoms and in this sense the Swahili Kingdoms became the main middle-men for trade between Great Zimbabwe, Arabia and Asia.

The Trans-Saharan Trade Route

The Trans-Saharan Trade Route refers to the interconnected set of trade routes which linked kingdoms between West Africa, North Africa and East Africa across the region of the Sahara in Africa. The water oasis dotted across the Sahara at the time provided resting and re-fueling places for the African traders. The Africans had established the Trans-Saharan trad route by 500 AD and from then onwards it simply expanded to encompass greater and greater territory. The Africans utilized caravans of camels to transport their good to different kingdoms and empires. The Trans-Saharan trade route transported goods such as salt, gold, copper, kola nuts, fruits, linen, cloth, glass. The Empire of Ghana by 800 AD completely controlled the gold trade from Ghana in the west up to northern Africa. Later the Empire of Mali took over the gold trade and established the trading centers of Timbuktu and Djenne.

The city of Timbuktu became one of the book trading centers of the world at this time. From Timbuktu trade took place across the Sahara near to the town of Takedda (modern-day Niger) which was later controlled by the Mali Empire. Takedda became well known for producing copper and a route from Tekedda across near the Tibesti Mountains (modern-day northern Chad) east to the city of Cairo (modern-day Egypt) was created. From the Hausa Kingdoms of western Africa (modern-day northern Nigeria) established trade routes from their region to the capital city of Kanem Empire named Njimi (modern-day Chad and Niger). Trade routes from the Kanem Empire north to the city of Tripoli (modern-day Libya) became popular. From Libya (modern-day Libya) a north-eastern trade route to the city of Egypt. In northern Africa, trade routes from Marrakesh (modern-day eastern Morocco) to Fez (modern-day northern Morocco) across to Qayrawan (modern-day Tunisia) ending in Libya were created.

Africa in the Torah

Within the holy book of the Jewish religion called the Torah which was written in around 600 BC we find several references to Africa and African people some of which are listed below:

Genesis Chapter 2: 10

> "A river watering the garden flowed from Eden; from there it was separated into four headwaters. The name of the first is the Pishon; it winds through the entire land of Havilah, where there is gold. The gold of that land is good; aromatic resin and onyx are also there. The name of the second river is the Gihon; it winds through the entire land of Cush". *(Cush is a kingdom is East Africa).*

Genesis: Chapter 12: 10

> "Now there was a famine in the land, and Abram went down to Egypt to live there for a while because the famine was severe". *(Egypt is located in North East Africa).*

Genesis: Chapter 16: 1

> "Now Sarai, Abram's wife, had borne him no children. But she had an Egyptian maidservant named Hagar". *(Hagar was an Egyptian).*

Genesis: Chapter 41: 45

> "Pharaoh gave Joseph the name Zaphenath-Paneah and gave him Asenath daughter of Potiphera priest of On." *(both Asenath and Potiphera were Egyptians).*

Genesis Chapter 10: 6

"The sons of Ham: Cush, Egypt, Put and Canaan". *(It is understood that Ham and his sons were all African).*

Genesis Chapter 10: 8

"Cush fathered Nimrod, he was the first on earth to be a mighty man. He was a mighty hunter before the Lord". *(Nimrod was an African).*

Africa in the Old Testament Bible

Within the holy book of the Christian religion called the Old Testament which was written in around 300 BC we find several references to Africa and African people some of which are listed below:

2 Kings: Chapter 19:9

"Now Sennacherib received a report that Tirhakah the King of Cush, was marching out to fight against him. So he again sent messengers to Hezekiah with this word". *(Tirhakah was an African King from the Nubian Empire).*

1 Kings: Chapter 10:1

"When the Queen of Sheba heard about the fame of Solomon and his relationship to the Lord, she came to test Solomon with hard questions" *(The Queen of Sheba was African).*

Jeremiah 38: 7

"But Ebed-Melech, a Cushite, an official in the royal palace, heard that they had put Jeremiah into cistern" *(Ebed-Melech was an African from Nubia).*

Numbers: Chapter 12: 1

"Miriam and Aaron began to talk against Moses because of his Cushite wife, for he had married a Cushite." *(Cushite is another name for the people of Kush or Cush who were Nubians).*

Zephaniah: Chapter 3: 10

"From beyond the rivers of Cush my worshipers, my scattered people, will bring me offerings." *(Cush or Kush is a reference to Nubia).*

2 Chronicles: Chapter 14:9

Zerah the Cushite marched out against them with an army of thousands upon thousands and three hundred chariots, and came as far as Mareshah. *(Zerah was an African military leader).*

Psalm: Chapter 68: 31

Nobles shall come from Egypt; Cush shall hasten to stretch out her hands to God. *(Egypt and Cush were kingdoms in Africa.*

Africa in the New Testament Bible

Within the holy book of the Christian religion called the New Testament which was written in around 150 AD we find several references to Africa and African people some of which are listed below:

Acts: Chapter 8:27

"And he rose and went. And there was an Ethiopian, a eunuch, a court official of Candace, Queen of the Ethiopians, who was in charge of all her treasure". *(Candace was an African Queen)*

Luke: Chapter 23:26

"As the soldiers led him away, they seized Simon from Cyrene, who was not from the country, and put the cross on him and made him carry it behind Jesus" *(Simon was an African from Libya, North Africa).*

Nahum: Chapter 3:8

"Are you better than Thebes, situated on the Nile, with water around her? The river was her defense, the waters her wall. Cush and Egypt were her boundless strength; Put and Libya were among her" *(Cush, Egypt, Punt also known as Somalia and Libya were all kingdoms in Africa)*

2 Chronicles: Chapter 12: 3

"Were not the Ethiopians and the Libyans a huge army with very many chariots and horsemen?" *(Ethiopia and Libya were both African kingdoms).*

Daniel Chapter 11: 43

"He will gain control of the treasures of gold and silver and all the riches of Egypt, with Libyans and Cushite's in submission. *(Egypt, Libya and Cush were all African Kingdoms)*

Africa in the Quran and Hadith

Within the holy book of the Islamic religion called the Quran which was written in around 645 AD. The Hadith are the collection of books regarding the Prophet Muhammed. We find several references to Africa and African people some of which are listed below:

Surah 31: Luqman: Verse 12

"We bestowed (in the past) wisdom on Luqman, 'Show (thy) gratitude to Allah'. Any who is grateful does so to the profit of his own soul; but if any is ungrateful, verily Allah is free of all wants, worthy of all praise".

(Luqman, also known as Luqman the Wise, was an African from Ethiopia).

Surah 27: Al Naml: Verse 29

"(The Queen of Sheba) said; 'Ye chiefs! Here is delivered to me a letter worthy of respect. It is from Solomon, and is (as follows): 'In the name of Allah, Most Gracious, Most Merciful: Be ye not arrogant against me, but come to me in submission (To the true religion)."

(The Queen of Sheba was an African Queen from Ethiopia).

African Proverb

"He who knows much speaks with silence".

CHAPTER 2

Ancient Archaeological Sites in Early Africa

The ancient Africans were skilled architects and builders who used the natural resources within the continent to construct castles, fortresses, temples and housing for their kingdoms. Ancient archaeological sites are scattered across the continent providing an insight into the history of each region. Below are some examples of well-known African archaeological sites:

Site 1: Southern Africa: Adams Calendar, Zimbabwe

Adams Calendar is a stone structure in southern African located in modern-day Zimbabwe. The stone structures are circular in design and date back 75,000 BC making them the oldest stone structures in the world. In addition, the stone structures appear to track he movement of the sun and are geographically aligned to equinoxes and solstices.

Site 2: Eastern Africa: Affad 23, Sudan

Affad 23 is an archaeological site in eastern African located in modern-day Sudan. The location consists of stone houses which date back to 15,000 BC and are evidence of early African habitations.

Site 3: North Central Africa: Gobero, Niger

Gobero is an archeological site in North Central Africa located in modern-day Niger. The location is home to one of the oldest graveyards in the Sahara region of Africa. A total of eight site comprise Gobero they date back to 8000 BC. The graveyards contain the remains of early Africans and also the remains of homes have been found there.

Site 4: West Africa, Stone Circles of Senegambia, Gambia

The Stone Circles of Senegambia is an archaeological site in West Africa located between the River Gambia and River Senegal. There are over 1000 monuments organized into 4 large stone circles. The stones are 2 metres in height and weigh up to 7 tons each. The site dates back to 300 BC.

Site 5: West Africa: Ruins of Loropeni, Cote d'Ivoire

The Ruins of Loropeni are an archaeological site in western Africa in modern-day Cote'd Ivoire on the borders of Togo and Ghana. The stone wall structures were developed in 1100 AD and number about 100 in total. In addition to the Ruins of Loropeni the region itself contains a further 10 fortresses. Loropeni was a west African town which is 11,130 square metres in size and used as part of the trans-Saharan gold trade.

Site 6: East Africa: Wargaade Wall, Somalia

The Wargaade Wall is an archaeological site in eastern Africa located in modern-day Somalia. The area in ancient times was also known as the Kingdom of Punt and is referred to in the Old Testament Bible. The Wargaade Wall is constructed of stone and the area has been excavated to reveal pottery and the graves of the Africans in this region.

Site 8: South Africa: Matobo Hills, Zimbabwe

The Matobo Hills are an archaeological site in southern Africa located in modern day Zimbabwe. The Motabo Hills have some of the highest concentrations of rock art in southern Africa and date back to 13,000 BC. The rock paintings had oil applied to them by the Africans that created them and presented the environment of the region inclusive of animals.

Site 9: West Africa Rhami Ruins, Zimbabwe

The Rhami Ruins are an archaeological site in southern Africa located in modern-day Zimbabwe. The location of the Rhami Ruins is the same site as the former capital of the Kingdom of Butwa rose to power in the region after the kingdom of Great Zimbabwe declined. The Kingdom of Butwa, who were related to the Shona people constructed the capital called Khami in 1450 BC from stone.

Site 10: East Africa: Aksum, Ethiopia

Aksum is an archaeological site in eastern Africa located in modern-day Ethiopia. The Kingdom of Aksum also known as the Ethiopian Empire constructed the City of Aksum in 100 AD. The Ethiopians constructed various towers, homes, churches, tombs, underground structures and obelisks some as high as 33 metres within the city.

Site 11: East Africa: Kondoa Rock-Art Sites, Tanzania

The Kondoa Rock Art site is an archaeological site located in eastern Africa in modern-day Tanzania. The Kondoa Rock area consists of 450 caves and rock shelters which contain rock paintings developed by the Africans in the region. The paintings dated back to about 50,000 BC. The paintings and rock art depict the local environment including but not limited to animals and hunting scenarios involving the Africans themselves.

African Proverb

"It is better to be a lion for a day than sheep all your life".

CHAPTER 3

Ancient Pre-Dynastic Cultures in East Africa

In north-eastern Africa numerous cultures and peoples developed prior to the eventual formation of the Nubian Empire and the Egyptian Empire. These African kingdoms and cultures were numerous and usually had specific characteristics with each culture building on the knowledge of the previous one and gradually growing in sophistication. The main cultures which developed in the area known as modern day Sudan and Egypt include the Halfan Culture, Qadan Culture, Faiyum Culture, Merimde Culture, Maadi Culture, Tasian Culture and the Badarian Culture. These cultures were then followed by the establishment of the Naqada Kingdoms. The period of time which all of the cultures cover is approximately 14,000 years and dates back from about 18,000 BC to 4800 BC which is when the Nubian Empire was established and later the Egyptian Empire in 3100 BC.

The Halfan Culture

The Halfan culture which was established in 18,000 BC. This African culture produced rock paintings and artifacts. Stone tools used by these peoples have been discovered by archeologists. Theses Africans developed their culture along the Nile River in north eastern area Africa. The Halfan culture were some of the earliest developers in the world of micro blade technologies which are very small stone blades used for chipping at stone and also flake tools which were a larger stone tool. The Halfan were engaged in fishing and also the consumption of heard animals for their food.

The Qadan Culture

Next, the Qadan Culture was established. These Africans operated within the region from 13,000 BC to 9,000 BC and are well known for hunting. The Qadan Culture controlled the same region as their predecessors the Halfan Culture namely modern-day northern Sudan. The ancient African cemetery known as Jebel Sahaba or Site 117 was discovered by archeologists in 1964 and contained the bodies of 59 Africans from the Qadan Culture.

The Faiyum Culture

The next African group within this region was the Faiyum Culture. The Faiyum Culture controlled the region from around 8000 BC to 5000 BC. This culture's territory extended to modern-day northern Egypt up to the area known as Lake Qarun. This culture produced a very heavily agricultural economy buying and selling produce in large quantities. Archeologists have also discovered at the location known as Site IX/81 remains of sheep, goat and cattle indicating the utilization of domesticated livestock. In addition, remains of turtles and crocodiles were discovered.

The Merimde Culture

The Merimde Culture was established in around 4800 BC and controlled the region which is west of the Nile River in the area known as Lower Egypt (Northern Egypt). A site which contained many artifacts of these Africans was discovered by archeologists in 1928 AD. Like their predecessors this group had an economy dominated by agriculture. However, there were differences between them and their predecessors like the Faiyum in that these groups did not bury their dead in separate cemeteries but rather within the same area as their own housing settlements.

The Maadi Culture

The Maadi Culture was established in 3900 BC and their territory covered Lower Egypt. It is worth noting that down to the south in modern-day Sudan at around the same time the Naqada Culture was also being established. The name Maadi is also the name of the archeological site in Lower Egypt where the majority of the artifacts which relate to these Africans were located. Again we find that the Maadi were heavily involved in agriculture and cultivated wheat, barley, lentils and peas. The remains found in the excavation sites included those of cattle, goats and sheep, but in addition donkeys and it is assumed that donkeys had been domesticated by the Maadi by this time.

The Tasian Culture

The Tasian culture was established in 4500 BC and this group controlled the Upper Egypt (south Egypt) area. The Tasian Culture of Upper Egypt and the Merimde Culture of Lower Egypt were therefore operating at around the same time. A key site where artifacts from the Tasian Culture were located on the east bank of the Nile River at a location called Deir Tasa. This African culture produced red and brown pottery that was painted black on the top and within the interior.

The Badarian Culture

The Badarian Culture was established around 4400 BC in south Egypt and it is likely that this culture overlapped somewhat with the Tasian Culture. In the 1920's archeologists discovered artifacts from this culture near a site called Al Badari. The Badarian Culture continued to created pottery in the style of their predecessors using the signature black top, however their technical precision was improved and pottery was often extremely thin walled. Upon excavation of the site over 600 graves were discovered and it is worth noting that there is evidence to suggest that more prosperous members of the community were buried in a separate area, this infers some social hierarchy being firmly established. It is understood by historians that the Badarian Culture predated the Naqada Culture by several centuries but there may have been some overlap. Environmental changes within the region to a drier climate ensured that these Africans migrated with their domesticated animals to more reliable lands which provided better watering facilities.

African Proverb

"Wealth is sharper than a sword".

CHAPTER 4

The Naqada Kingdoms

The Naqada Kingdom were Africans who established themselves prior to the formation of the first dynasties of the Egyptian Empire in the north east region of Africa and they are the people from which the Egyptian Empire descended. The Naqada Kingdoms are generally divided into 3 sections namely Nadada 1, Naqada 2 and Naqada 3 the first of which began in around 4000 BC.

Naqada 1

The first Naqada Kingdoms were established in around 4000 BC. The Naqada Culture descended from their predecessors the Badarian Culture and as a consequence archeologists found that much of their pottery carried much of the same characteristics namely the black topped brown pottery. We find also evidence of structured society with elite members of the group being buried within a separate area. One of the well-known cemeteries of this group is known by historians as Cemetery T and this site displayed tombs that were larger in size. Areas which had contained no burials have been found near an area known as Nubt and later numerous gold mines near to this region and in Nubia have also been located. Naqada 1 is also sometimes known as the Amaratian Culture which derives its name from an archaeological site known as El Amra. At this time, we also know that Naqada located in Upper Egypt traded with the Africans in Lower Egypt. Mud brick buildings were developed during this period. We also have evidence that deceased persons were buried with food, weapons and vases indicating a strong belief in the afterlife.

Naqada 2

The Naqada 2 Kingdoms were established 3500 BC; this culture is also known as the Gerzeh Culture deriving its name from the Gerzeh cemetery located on the west bank of the Nile River in Egypt. New pottery known as Marl is also developed at this and its characteristics include a rough surface with a pale green, grey and white color on the artifacts. Metal development is also characteristic of this period, stone vessels and flint knives were also created and used during this time. Some of the pottery of this period was decorated with boats, oars and always flamingos.

Naqada 3

The Naqada 3 Kingdoms were established in around 3200 BC, this group of Africans constructed the first royal cemeteries, elite only burial places and also continued with the mud-brick architecture. In this period the first state rulers were established and formal kingship. In addition, this period signified the increased use of copper and also the continuation of decorated pottery. The earliest hieroglyphic representations were also established at this time. Hieroglyphics would later become the formalized written language of their descendants the Egyptian Dynasties.

African Proverb

"He who refuses to obey cannot command".

CHAPTER 5

The Nubian Empire: Part 1

The Nubian Empire was established in around 4800 BC. The Nubian Empire was located in north-eastern Africa in the area which is today know as Sudan. Later the capitals of the Nubian Empire would be Kerma, Napata and Meroe. It has been suggested that the origin of the word 'Nubia' might be *nbw*, the Egyptian word for gold. It is understood by historians that the Nubians were the original ancestors and predecessors of what would later become Ancient Egypt which was located to the north of Sudan. Although the Nubians and the Egyptians were of the same race they had different cultures. A famous text named the Edfu Text details the origin of ancient Egypt and states that civilization was brought from the south (Ancient Nubia). In addition, the ancient Egyptian god Osiris is thought to have originated in Nubia and this was documented by the Greek Historian Diodorius Siculus. This notion is further supported in the Egyptian text named Leyden Papyrus where Osiris is described as a Nubian God, and also the gods Isis and Set, Amen-Ra, Hathor and Nut. The Nubians are well known to have developed the world's first astronomical devices which were used to track calendars, positioning of the stars and the solstices. A solstice is an astronomical event that occurs twice each year as the Sun reaches its highest or lowest points. The remains of these astronomical deviced were found in an area called Nabta. The Nubian lived along the southern sections of the Nile River in north-east Africa. The farming community of the Nubian Empire grew lentils, peas, melons and dates. In addition, the Nubians mined for gold and other minerals such as carnelian. The Nubians had also had a community of herdsmen who managed cattle and developed animal skins for trade. One of the main trading partners of the Nubians were their neighbours to the north the Naqadan Egyptians and they also traded with Palestine. Later the Nubians developed writing systems and the Merotic language. Eventually the Nubian Empire would expand its territory and ultimately conquer Egypt.

Nubian A and B Group

The early Nubian Empire is catergorized by historians and archeologists as being divided into three groups namely the A-Group, B-Group and C-Group beginning in around 4800 BC. The A-Group was an early culture that developed between the 1st and 2nd Cataract in the area known as Lower Nubia which is geographically to the North of Nubia. The Nubian A Group and B Group are usually grouped together and overlapped in their timeline. The Nubians grew in power and influence in the region due to trade. The Nubian A Group and B Group controlled Nubia at the same time as Naqada 3 was operating in southern Egypt also known as Upper Egypt. One of the important cemetaries of the A-Group and B-Group was located in the region called Qustul above the 2nd Cataract in modern day Sudan. Within the area of Lower Nubia excavations have found remnants of stone houses with between 2 and 6 rooms and fireplaces and also elite burial grounds. The elite burial grounds were mainly used for kings, their families and court members. Females and males were buried together at times and also females with children along with gold. The Nubians were very strong believers in the afterlife and often buried their deceased with pottery, gold, jewellery, bowls, tools and linen clothing. Male Nubian burials have also been found with their bows and arrows which were adorned with ostrich feather plumes. There was evidence of trade between the Nubian A-Group and B-Group and also the Naqada Culture. Hunting and fishing were practiced by theses Africans and the food produced at this time included barley, wheat and leguminous plants.

Nubian C Group

The Nubian C Group developed in around 2300 BC and are the direct decendants of the A-Group and B-Group. The early settlements were establised in the areas of Lower Nubia known as Faras, Dakka and Aniba. The C-Group were known for building circular structures filled with sand and gravel and later mud brick. Multiple circular housing structures have been found in the Aniba area. In similar fashion to their predecesssors, the Nubian C-Group again were farmers and herders. From Egyptian records we know that further to the south the Kerma Culture was also established at around the same time and developed into a powerhouse in the region later. Again as with the previous A-Group and B-Group trade continued between Nubia and Egypt and it was not uncommon for Nubians to be soldiers within the Egyptian Armies. Nubians were buried with their heads facing to the east and with gold, jewelry and linen and leather garments.

Trade Between Early Nubia and Early Naqada

As elluded to earlier the ancient Nubian A, B and C group kindgoms in southern part of north east africa (modern-day Sudan) were established and functioning simulatenously with the Naqada I, II and III kingdoms in the northern part of north-east Africa (modern-day Egypt). As a consquence the evidence suggests that there was significant trade between the two african nations. This fact is evidenced and verified by the analysis of the gaves and cemetries of both cultures from this time each of which were located to some extent along the Nile River which was utilized at times as a transport vehicle. Excavation of cemeteries in the area of Nubia named Qutsul and excavation in the area of Egypt called Naga-ed Der have both revealed interesting data on the artifacts. Nubian cemeteries contain palettes from Naqada as well as beads and gaming boards and mace heads. Upon analyis of the Nubians graves it was uncovered that over time Naqada goods increased suggesting that trade between the two nations grew stronger. Due to its geographical location Nubia also controlled the import of goods from central Africa. Nubia was abundant in gold and also typically supplied Naqada with ivory and ostrich feathers and also wood from other African regions. Naqada had excellent soil at the time and provided wheat to Nubia. Trade would continue between the two nations and they both expanded into the Dynasties of Egypt and the Kindgom of Kush respectively.

Ancient Kingdom of Kerma

The Nubians established the Kerma Culture was in 2500 BC and it was also known as Dukki Gel. The capital of the Kerma culture was the city of Kerma. Between 2500 BC and 1500 BC the city had a population of around 10,000 inhabitants and began to organize labour for large structures, walls and palaces. The Kerma Culture eventually unified the region into one kingdom making it one of the earliest urbanized communities in the world. The Kingdom of Kerma controlled both Upper and Lower Nubia. The Kerma Culture is usually divided by historians into 3 periods namely Early Kerma (2500-2000 BC), Middle Kerma (2000-1750 BC) and Classic Kerma (1750-1480 BC). In Early Kerma the kingdom controlled just Upper Nubia. The period corresponds to the 11th, and 12th Dynasties of Egypt and was temporarily at war with their neighbours the Egyptians. Classic Kerma corresponds with the 13th Dynasty of Egypt and by this time Nubia was fully unified. Two notable Kerman Kings were King Awana and King Nedjeh.

The Kerma Culture controlled a region from the 1st cataract to the 4th cataract which means that the size of the territory was equal to that of Egypt. As a consequence, the Egyptians gradually grew to view the Kerma Culture and the latter Kush Empire as growing threat. At this time the growing power of Kerma in this region encouraged the Egyptians to safeguard their territory to the south by building fortresses around the 2nd and 3rd cataracts which bordered the area just north of Kerma. The capital city Kerma was surrounded by villages and as in the case of their direct ancestors the A, B, and C-Group continued to cultivate the land, and also hunt and mine for gold and other precious metals. About 4 kilometres east of the main city around 30,000 burials have been located and these include 4 royals' tombs where royals were buried. The Nubians of Kerma established trade roots into other regions of the African continent and the Mediterranean and this increased the wealth of the city.

A stele is an upright large stone slab erected as a monument. Three large stele have been discovered in the royal cemetery of Kerma. The geographical location of the city meant that the Africans of Kerma became a gateway for trade between the continent of Africa, Middle-east and Mediterranean Europe. The Nubians of Kerma established the island of Sai (located in the Nile river between the 3rd and 2nd Cataracts) as a major trading post for their gold, ivory, copper, ostrich feathers, fruits, and exotic animals. The Hyksos were an Asiatic people from western Asia who in around 1500 BC were attempting to attack and conquer the entire area of Egypt. At this time Hyksos has already successfully taken control of some regions of northern (Lower) Egypt and this was the first time in history that a foreign nation had successfully controlled any part of north-eastern Africa. The Hyksos devised a plan and tried to approach the Nubians of Kerma with a plan to jointly attack Egypt, the Hyksos would attack Egypt from the north while the Nubians of Kerma would attack Egypt from the south simultaneously.

However, Pharaoh Kamose of the 17th Dynasty of Egypt found out about the plan and attacked the Hyksos. The Hyksos appealed to the Nubian Kings of Kerma for help and rock inscriptions found at the area called Arminna in Nubia describe some events of this period. Up until this point Kerma had been a trading partner with Egypt. Pharaoh Kamose launched two military campaigns against the Kerma Culture. Upon the death of Pharaoh Kamose his brother Pharaoh continued the war with Nubia and eventually gained control of many of the gold mines. The Nubian gold production made Egypt a prime source of gold in the region and they became the wealthiest empire in the world at this time. One of the oldest maps known is of a gold mine in Nubia called The Turin Papyrus Map. By 1490 BC the Kerma Culture were carrying out regular military attacks against Egypt and by 1100 BC the Egyptians had been driven out of Nubia completely.

African Proverb

"Do not look where you fell, but where you slipped".

CHAPTER 6

The Nubia Kingdom of Kush

The Kingdom of Kush was established in 1070 BC in the area known as Ancient Nubia which is in modern-day Sudan. The word "Kush" was used by the ancient Egyptians for this kingdom and is also sometimes referred to as 'The Cush Empire'. The Kingdom of Kush is also referenced in the Christian Biblical Book of Jasher with the following verse:

"So Kikianus king of Cush (Kush) went forth with all the children of Cush, a people numerous as the sand, and he went to fight against Aram and the children of the east, to bring them under subjugation." (Book of Jasher, Chapter 72, Verse 2)."

The first capital of the Kingdom of Kush was established as the city of Napata which was located south of Kerma between the 4th and 5th Cataract. By the year 800 BC the capital city of Napata was thriving. The major conquests of the Kushite Empire had its beginning with the first ruler King Alara, whose wife was Queen Kasaka. King Alara unified Nubia and was documented within Egyptian hieroglyphics. The Kushite Kings also had the title 'King of the Upper and Lower Nubia'.

Life in the Kingdom of Kush

The people of Kush were known to be extremely religious. Nicolaus of Damascus was a Greek historian who lived during the reign of the Roman Empire. Upon research of the Kingdom of Kush Nicolaus of Damascus mentioned that:

"They cultivate piety and righteousness. Their houses have no doors, and although there are many items left lying in the streets, no one ever steals them".

The role of women within the Kush kingdom was also unique in the ancient world in the sense that they played a key role in the governance of the kingdom. The Kushite women used henna to beautify themselves and a powder called kohl to paint their eyelids. The Kushite women also wore jewellery including necklaces, anklets and earrings. Like their predecessors the people of Kush were farmers and also raised animals. The Kushite's kept domesticated cattle, goats, sheep and horses. Agatharchidus of Cnidus was a Greek historian who commented that the Kushite's were extremely skilled herdsmen, he mentioned that:

"the Kush herdsmen possess a large number of animals which accompany them, they hang cowbells from the horns of all the males in order that their sound might drive off wild beasts. At nightfall, they collect their herds into barns and cover these with hurdles made from palm branches. Their women and children mount up on top of these. The men, however light fires in a circle and sing traditional tales and thus ward off to sleep".

The Kushite's generated income through their agricultural activities and this was made easier by the flooding of the Nile which enabled the irrigation of the local fields. In addition, the trade of gold ivory, ostrich eggs and aromatic woods from the interior of Africa also provided additional income. Strabo was a Greek philosophers and historian who travelled to Kush and mentioned that:

"in the towns the dwellings are made of material split from palm trees as well as mud bricks".

The Kingdom of Kush developed numerous wall paintings, statues, pottery and engravings that depict life in Kush. Some of the paintings show female Kushite dancers who took part in Kushite religious ceremonies. The Kushite's also made and played musical instruments including drums, flutes and horns all of which are also depicted within the wall paintings.

The Deffufa

The Deffufa is a unique structure in Kushite architecture, it was a large mud brick temple used by the elite of Kush. There are three Deffufa located in Nubia. The western Deffufa is a solid rectangular mass of mud brick more than 150 feet long and 75 feet wide. The walls of the Deffufa were decorated with tiles and gold leaf. The lower western Deffufa was used as a warehouse. The eastern Deffufa is slightly shorter than the western Deffufa was used as a funeral chapel. The third Deffufa is the smallest. The three Deffufa temples are unparalleled anywhere else in the ancient world.

The Kushite Army

The Kingdom of Kush produced many sandstone carvings some of which depicted the military conquests of the Kush army. Herodotus was a Greek historian who was born in the region which is now modern day Turkey. Herodotus when commenting on the armies of Kush mentioned "the Kushite's carried long bows not less than four cubits (2 meters) in length made from palm trees and on them they placed short arrows made of cane, when they go to battle they smear one half of their body with chalk and other half with red pigment". The Kush army also carried large shields made of animal hides.

The Kushite Conquest of Egypt

In around the year 747 BC The Kingdom of Kush conquered the entire region of Egypt and established themselves as the 25th Dynasty of Egypt. The Kushite King who lead the initial conquest of Egypt was King Kashta, his wife was the Queen Pebatjma and his brother was Alara the first recorded King of Nubia who unified Nubia and established the Kingdom of Kush. Just prior to the Nubian conquest of Egypt some Libyan kings had temporarily taken control over parts of Egypt and therefore Egypt was already in a weakened state. However, the Libyan kings were actually pawns of the Kingdom of Kush who were essentially already ruling Egypt by proxy. When the Libyans attempted to rebel against the more powerful Kingdom of Kush and become independent, the Kushite Kings decide to launch a full scale attack and conquer the entire land of Egypt.

One of the ways in which the Kingdom of Kush promoted and solidified their conquest of Egypt was by reminding the Egyptians that previously the lands of Nubia and Egypt were once one and that they were actually descended from the same peoples. The son of Kashta was King Piye and he continued the campaign and conquered Lower Egypt (northern Egypt) and this completed the Kushite invasion, occupation and control of Egypt establishing themselves as the 25th Dynasty of Egypt. The Kushite King Piye also known as Piankhi like the majority of the Kushite peoples was very religious and viewed the campaign as a holy war. King Piye would order his soldiers to cleanse themselves before going war. Upon his victory King Piye constructed the temple of Amun at Gebel Barkal.

The Kushite Religion

The Kushite's were a very religious African nation and had their own God, priests and temples with structured traditions and rites. The Kushite's established a class of priests which oversaw the temples and would provide guidance to the Kings and Queens of Kush. The main God that the Kushite's worshipped was Amun and was considered the creator of everything in existence.

The religious centre for the Kingdom of Kush was Gebel Barkal where three palaces and thirteen temples were also located. The peoples of the Kingdom of Kush also worshipped Egyptian deities which had been introduced to Nubia prior to the Kushite conquest of Egypt. The key Gods and Goddesses of the Kingdom of Kush included:

1. **Amun** – The creator of everything in existence.
2. **Apedemak** – Warrior god associated with the moon.
3. **Arensnuphis** – The god of air and wind
4. **Bastet** – The goddess associated with motherhood
5. **Bes** – The protector god of dancing and singing
6. **Hathor** – The goddess of love and beauty and protector of women in childbirth
7. **Horus** – The son of the Egyptian sun god Re
8. **Isis** – The protector goddess of the dead
9. **Ma'at** – The goddess of balance and harmony which regulates the stars and seasons
10. **Osiris** – The god associated with dead rulers
11. **Ptah** – The god of artists
12. **Sekhmet** – The goddess for chaos and anger
13. **Taueret** – The protector goddess of women

One of the reasons that Kushite leadership continued to worship some Egyptian gods and goddesses is that it provided some legitimacy to their control and rule over Egypt. It was therefore a strategic and political tool used to unify the region and peoples. There were some differences in terms of depictions, for example in Kush the god Amun was depicted with a ram's head whereas in Egypt Amun was represented in human form.

The Kings and Queens of Kush

The Kingdom of Kush produced a long line of well renowned Kings and Queens. The Kings were known as King or Pharaoh as in the case when Kush controlled Egypt and the Queens often had the title Kandrake which in English means "mother of the prince".

King Alara: 795 BC to 760 BC

King Alara is credited as being the founder Kush and the first recorded King of the Kingdom of Kush. King Alara unified the Kingdom of Kush and established it as a powerful empire. King Alara also established Napata as the new capital of the Kingdom of Kush. King Alara was documented in Egyptian hieroglyphics.

King Kashta: 760 BC to 747 BC

King Kashta was the brother of King Alara and launched the initial attacks against Egypt in a desire to conquer the entire region. King Kashta is credited with conquering the entire region of Upper Egypt (southern Egypt).

Pharaoh Piye: 742 BC to 721 BC

King Piye (also known as Piankhy) continued the invasion of Egypt and conquered all of Lower Egypt (northern Egypt). Once the conquest was complete King Piye returned to the capital of the Kingdom of Kush which at the time was Napata. King Piye is credited with completing the establishment of the 25th Dynasty of Egypt.

Pharaoh Shabaka: 721 BC to 707 BC

Pharaoh Shabaka (also known as King Shabaqo) was the brother of Pharaoh Piye and the 2nd Pharaoh of the 25th Dynasty of Egypt. Pharoah Shabaka moved to Egypt to establish tighter control over the region. Shabaka's managed to consolidated control over Egypt and made Thebes his capital. In Karnak he erected a statue of himself wearing the twin crowns of Egypt which symbolized Upper and Lower Egypt.

Pharaoh Shebitku: 707 BC to 690 BC

Pharaoh Shebitku was the 3rd Phararoh of the 25th Dynasty and his father was King Piye. Shebitku was engaged in numerous battles with the Assyrians (based in modern day Iraq). In order to defeat the Assyrians Shebitku aligned himself with the Kings of Israel.

Pharaoh Taharqa: 690 BC to 664 BC

Pharaoh Taharqa was the son of King Piye. At the early age of 20 Pharaoh Taharaqa led a Kushite and Egyptian army against the Assyrians who were at the time advancing against Jerusalem. Pharaoh Taharqa defeated the Assyrians.

Pharaoh Tanwetamani: 664 BC to 653 BC

Pharaoh Tanwetamani was the nephew of Pharaoh Taharqa and the son of Pharaoh Shebitku. Pharaoh Tanwetamani's royal name was Bakare which means "Glorious is the soul of Re".

King Aspelta: 600 BC to 580 BC

King Aspelta was selected by 24 military and religious leaders to be king and was crowned in Napata. The tomb of Aspelta was located in Nuri and is the second largest burial structure. King Aspelta was a great-grandson of Pharaoh Taharqa. After Napata was attacked by Egyptian forces around 591 BC King Aspelta established a royal court at Meroe.

King Irike-Amanote: 430 BC to 405 BC

King Irike-Amanote was crowned at Napata and was a warrior king who was known to seize and subdue surrounding lands. He conducted war against nomadic groups to the east and it is thought that he had aspirations to re-conquer the whole of Egypt. He also assisted Egypt in their battles against Persia.

King Harsiotef: 390 BC to 350 BC

King Harisotef ruled Kush longer than any other Kushite King and took on many titles based on the Egyptian titles such as Kanakht Khaemnpet (Mighty Bull appears in Napata) and Sameryamun (Beloved son of Amun). King Harsiotef's wife was a Nubian Queen named Queen Batahaliye who was buried in a pyramid named by archaeologists as pyramid Nu 44 which is inscribed with Egyptian hieroglyphs. King Harsiotef launched multiple military campaigns in the north in an effort to expand the influence of the Kushite Empire.

King Nastasen: 335 BC to 315 BC

King Nastasen is famed for successfully retaliating against invading forces from Egypt. In addition, he fought a number of successful battles against nomadic tribes. His reign is described on a stele (stone slab erected as a monument) located in Jebel Barkal. The mother of King Nastasen was Queen Pelkha.

Queen Shanakdakhete: 177BC to 155 BC

Queen Shanakdakhete is known as the first female ruler of the Kushite Empire. An inscription in Merotic hieroglyphics was found in what archaeologists call Temple F in Naga. The Merotic script was first developed in around 700 BC. Queen Shanakdakhete's pyramid was one of the largest ever built in Meroe.

Queen Amanirenas: 40 BC to 10 BC

Queen Amanirenas was one of the greatest queens of the Kush Empire and is famed for leading the Kushite Army against the Romans from 27 BC to 22 BC. Queen Amanirenas led an army of 30,000 Kushite soldiers and defeated the Romans who were stationed within the Egyptian cities of Aswan and Philae. The defeat of the Romans led to a peace treaty being created between Rome and Kush. Queen Amanirenas's husband was King Teriteqas and their son was the Prince Akinidad.

Queen Amanishakheto: 10 BC to 1AD

Queen Amanishakheto was known for her extreme wealth and power. Queen Amanishakheto constructed numerous temples and pyramids in the area known as Wad Ban Naqa in Meroe. The palace of Queen Amanishakheto had over 60 rooms and was also located in Meroe.

A large quantity of golden artifacts were stolen from her tomb by European grave robbers in the 1820 AD and sold to German museums. Queen Amanishakheto also defeated a Roman Army sent by the Roman emperor Augustus who attempted to break the peace treaty between Rome and Kush.

Queen Amanitore & King Natakamani: 1 AD to 20 AD

Queen Amanitore was married to King Natakamani. The royal palace was at Gebel Barkal located in modern day Sudan. Queen Amanitore and King Natakamani shared power during their twenty-year rule. Queen Amanitore was one of the last great builders and developed water reservoirs and restored the temple of Amun in Meroe.

African Proverb

"Do not set sail with another man's star".

CHAPTER 7

The Nubian Empire: Part 2

Nubia was home to three Kushite Kingdoms namely Kerma in which was established in 2500 BC. The second which was Napata was developed in 1000 BC and was flourishing by 800 BC and the third was Meroe which was developed in 300 BC and lasted to 300 AD.

The Nubian Pyramids

The Nubians began the construction of their pyramids from 747 BC until around 300 AD. It is understood that King Kashta began the construction of the Nubian Pyramids and eventually 255 pyramids were created by these Africans, the earliest of which was at a location known as El-Kurru. Many of the pyramids contained tombs for the Nubian Kings and also the Nubian warrior Queens. The location with the largest number of pyramids was at Meroe and includes burials for over 40 Kings and Queens. The Nubian Pyramids differ from the Egyptian Pyramids in numerous ways, firstly the Nubians constructed a larger number of pyramids. Secondly, the Nubian Pyramids are smaller in structure and typically range from six to thirty metres in height. The development of the Nubian pyramids may also have been an attempt to integrate the two nations of the Nubians and Egyptians. The Nubian Pyramids are a more recent creation than their Egyptian counterparts.

The Pyramids of El-Kurru

The Nubian Pyramids of El-Kurru are located on the right bank of the Nile River and the location was utilized as a cemetery by the royal families of the Nubians. The pyramids also house the tombs of King Piankhi and King Shabaka. The pyramid of King Piankhi has a base length of 8 metres and a stairway which consists of 19 steps. There were also 14 queen's pyramids located here including Queen Tabiry, Queen Nefrukekashta, Queen Peksater, Queen Naparaye, Queen Khensa and Queen Qalhata.

The Pyramids of Nuri

The Nubian Pyramids of Nuri houses the tombs of 21 kings and 52 queens and princess. Some of the royal family of Nubia buried here include King Taharqa, King Amaniastabarqa, King Aspelta, King Talakhamani, King Harsiotef, King Nastasen, King Malewiebamani and King Analmaye. The pyramids at Nuri are much larger than the pyramids of El-Kurru. The pyramid of Taharqa was 50 metres high.

The Pyramids of Meroe

The Nubian Pyramids of Meroe were created from sandstone house three royal cemeteries namely the South Cemetery, the West Cemetery and the North Cemetery. The South Cemetery consists of 195 tombs as well as pyramids. The South Cemetery of Meroe contains a total of nine royal pyramids. The site contains the tombs of King Amanislo, King Anlamani and King Siaspiqa. The West Cemetery consists of 113 tombs and is a non-royal burial ground. The North Cemetery consists of 41 royal pyramids and includes the burial sites for Queen Amanitore, King Amanikhabale, Queen Amanishakheto, King Tarekeniwal and King Natakamani.

The Pyramids of Sedeinga

The Nubian Pyramids of Sedeinga are an archeological site in modern-day Sudan which was also constructed by the Nubians. The site which is located west of the River Nile and north of Meroe contains 35 pyramids many of which were constructed with a circle inside of them. The site when excavated in 2012 AD contained pottery, jewellery, amulets, and artifacts decorated with the Meroitic writing.

The Nabta Playa and Astronomy in Ancient Nubia

As we mentioned previously The Nabta Playa is the world's oldest astronomical observatory. The Nabta Playa is located in near Nabta in the Nubian desert in East Africa. This astronomical observatory dates back to around 4800 BC. Utilizing satellite imagery, scientists have identified that other parts of the structure align to the constellation called 'Ursa Major' (also known as the Great Bear) and were used to track 'azimuth's'. An azimuth is a measurement of the arc of a horizon measured clockwise from the south point. In addition, the azimuth of the Sirius star system and also stars from Orion's belt were also tracked.

The Capital City of Napata

By 750 BC the capital of Kush was moved from Kerma to Napata. Napata is located near fourth cataract in the southernmost part of Nubia. The Kushite Empire which was inclusive of the 25th dynasty of Egypt considered Napata the capital of the kingdom and this is the place where the kings were crowned. King Alara established Napata as the religious centre of Nubia. The Nubian King Piye was known for being very pious, avoiding bloodshed and being extremely religious. King Piye established Napata as the capital of Nubia and began the construction of temples. Even after the capital had moved to Meroe, Napata remained the coronation city. There was a temple of Gebel Barkal near Napata which is a place where many of the religious ceremonies were conducted. Napata remained a key centre point until around 590 BC and much of the economy over this period in Napata was based on gold which was an abundant commodity in the region. The main diety in the region during this time was Amun. Eventually the capital was moved to Meroe.

The Capital City of Meroe

The last capital of the Nubian Empire was Meroe and was formally established in around 300 BC and flourished until 400 AD. The city of Meroe was located on the east bank of Nile River near modern day Shendi in Sudan in East Africa and was a very well organised and powerful African state. The city of Meroe was south of the former capital city for the Nubians of Napata. It is also worth noting that over time the capital cities of the Nubian moved ever more south deeper into Africa. Meroe is also the location of the majority of the pyramids constructed by the Nubians. In Biblical tradition it is known that the prophet Moses later married a Nubian woman from the region which is mentioned in the book of Numbers in the Christian Bible. Although there was no clear cultural break from the Napatan period upon the establishment of Mero a new religious cult was developed around the warrior diety Apedemak and some new temples were created. The Egyptian name for Apedemak was Pa-ir-meki which translates into English as "the one who protects".

From a strategic perspective the region of Moreo provided some protection from foreign invaders because of Nile and Atbara rivers near it. The region had an abundance of iron ore and hardwood. One of the unique aspects of Meriotic Nubia was the fact that priests controlled a large amount of the political power in the country and often monarchs were recalled or replaced by them. Women were often matriarchs and would rule the nation while a male heir was growing up. As a consequence, queens were often depicted in murial's as equals of the king, standing alongside him or in the process of conquering the enemy. Meroe eventually became a major trading centre in the region for gold, ivory, animal skins, ostrich feathers, slaves and iron. Iron smelting in Meroe became a very large industry so much so that the British researcher Archibald Sayce upon publishing his report after completing his excavation of Meroe in the early 1900's remarked the following:

"Meroe in fact, must have been the Birmingham of ancient Africa; the smoke of its iron-smelting furnace's must has been continually going up to heaven, and the whole of northern Africa might have been supplied by it with implements of iron".

It is likely that King Taharq may have deliberately initiated a large iron industry at Meroe after learning that the Assyrians had begun using iron weapons. Based on excavations at Meroe which took into account the smelting process, iron technologies, furnace sizes, it is now understood that about 10 tons of iron metal were produced each year. Another advantage of having the city in Meroe was the seasonal differences in that within the region there were summer rains which allowed these Africans to extend their farming activities. Millet and sorghum (a plant native to Africa) were cultivated and cattle raising was increased. The increase in food production further enabled the population of the kingdom to grow. The strengthening of trade was also supported by the unique geographical positon which provided a route to the Red Sea and access to Arabia and Eastern Asia. The Nubians were as a consequence able to sell their iron products into India.

The Merotic Language and Alphabet

The Nubians had first developed the Merotic script when the capital was at Kerma. By 700 BC during Napatan Period the language had been further developed. There were two forms of the Merotic Script namely the cursive form which was joined up handwriting and also the hieroglyphic form which utilized symbols and was written in columns from top to bottom. There were 23 letters in the Merotic alphabet inclusive of four vowels. By 300 BC the Nubians had fully developed the Merotic Language. The writings were often on papyrus and parchment. Papyrus paper is made from the pith (centre) of the papyrus plant which was abundant at the time in the east of Africa.

In 1819 AD, the French architect Franz Gau became one of the first Europeans to copy the Meroitic text when he reproduced a Nubian inscription found at The Temple of Dakka. Even earlier in Egyptian texts of the 18th dynasty we find the Meroitic language, such as an inscription which reads "beautiful is the Kushite". Also, in some their writings and also in the Egyptian Book of the Dead some Meroitic phrases are found. The last known writings of the Merotic writing are found in a temple column in Kalabsha which is in Lower Nubia and refer to the Nubian King Kharamadoye, these writings are thought to be dated at 420 AD.

War between the Nubian Empire and Rome

By 40 BC the Nubians had established an impressive standing military force equip with some of the best archers in the world at that time. The Queens of Nubia were known as Kandake's which was the name for queen in the merotic language. By 40 BC the Queen of Nubia was Amanirenas who ruled until 10 BC and her son was Prince Akinidad. Akinidad became the governor of Lower Nubia and carried out restoration and building in the area of Nubia named Kawa. The Romans who had conquered Egypt at this time attempted to impose taxes on the Nubians. In 24 BC Prince Akinidad led an army of 30,000 Nubian soldiers and reinforcements from central Africa against the Romans and defeated their forces which were located at the Egyptian cities of Aswan and Philae at that time. In addition, he also drove out the Jews who were located at Elephantine Island in Egypt. Queen Amanirenas and her son Prince Akinidad returned to Nubia with Roman slaves and treasure from the conquest of Rome. After this event a peace treaty was greed between the Nubian Empire and the Roman Empire and the previously imposed taxes were rescinded.

Queen Amanirenas was succeeded by Queen Amanishakheto who ruled from 10 BC to 1 AD. Queen Amanishakheto is depicted in monuments as having three scars below her left eye. By this time the Egyptian Empire to the north of Nubia had fallen to the Romans. The founder of the Roman Empire was Augustus Caesar and ruled from 27 BC to 14 AD. Augustus Caesar led the Roman Empire and began to encroach upon Nubian territory breaking a previous peace treaty between the two empires and in around 29 BC the Romans eventually attacked Nubia due to the Romans desire to take Wadi Allaqi which was rich in gold reserves. The Wadi was located in Lower Nubia. Under the leadership of the Nubian Queen Amanishakheto the Nubians attacked the Romans in Aswan and then led her army to Thebes and defeated the Roman Army. Once they defeated the Romans the Nubians enslaved the Romans and destroyed the statues of Caesar. The Nubians buried a statue under the floor of a temple at Meroe. In the belief system of the Nubians they believed that by stepping over a representation of their enemy the power of their enemy the Romans would be further weakened and destroyed.

Queen Amanishakheto is often depicted on Nubian murals as being covered with jewels and carrying weapons in her hands. Queen Amanishakheto was succeeded by Queen Amintore who was her daughter and she ruled from 1AD and had her royal palace at Gebel Barkal. This queen was known for rebuilding several temples in Wad ban Naqa located 80 kilometres from Napata and Meroe itself. The palace of Queen Amanishakheto located at Wad ban Naqa had 40 rooms and was decorated with gold. At the location of her palace were another 12 pyramids were constructed. Queen Amanisakheto was eventually buried in her own pyramid in Meroe. Sadly, in 1834 AD, the Italian treasure hunter Giuseppe Ferlini destroyed 40 Nubian pyramids and stole the numerous ancient African artifacts and treasures. By 320 AD the now powerful Ethiopian Empire to the south east lead by King Ezana had invaded Nubia and sacked Meroe and this event contributed to the eventual decline of the Nubian Empire.

The Kingdom of Makuria

The Kingdom of Makuria was established and grew in power and statue after the decline of the Nubian Empire in the years after 350 AD. Part of the decline of the Nubian Empire meant the breaking up of territories into smaller African kingdoms. The kingdom was located in the same region near to the former capital of Nubia which was Napata. The Kingdom of Makuria also had near to itself two other African kingdoms of Nubian descent namely Alwa (also known as Alodia) to the south and Nobadia (also known as Nobatia) to the north. The capital of Nobadia was Faras just south of Aswan in Egypt and the capital of Alwa was Soba which close to Khartoum in modern-day Sudan. The Africans of Makuria used mud-brick to build what would become the capital of Makuria called Old Dongola which was near to the Nile River between the neighbouring kingdoms of Alwa and Nobadia. By 600 BC the kingdom of Makuria and the kingdom of Nobadia combined to form a much larger kingdom and Christianity had been introduced.

The First Battle of Dongola

By 642 AD Islam had spread throughout the Middle-East and a Muslim nation known as the Rashidun Caliphate had been established with their capital being based in Medina, Arabia. The Rashidun Caliphate attempted to invade Nubia with an army of 20,000 Arab soldiers. The Kingdom of Makuria defeated them due to their superior military tactics which included the use of the bow and arrow. The Nubians had been known for thousands of years as skilful archers in fact the area had been named the 'Land of the Bow'. The invading Arab army were to experience the stunning precision of the Nubian archers first hand and suffer a devastating defeat as the Nubians of Makuria used horses and archers to launch attacks at incredible speed limiting the Arabs to form any coherent or lasting retaliation. The Arab army was defeated and they withdrew and a peace treaty between the two nations was agreed.

The Second Battle of Dongola

In 652 AD due to a breach of the peace treaty war erupted again between the two kingdoms. The Arabs were led by Abdallah Ibn Sa'd who declared war and marched 5000 Arab soldiers against the Africans of the Kingdom of Makuria. Yet again the Arab army was defeated and this time a peace treaty known as 'The Baqt' was established. The Islamic scholar Ibn Abd Al-Hakam records the following regarding the events:

"After that Abdallah signed a truce with them (the Nubians), as he was unable to defeat them".

The Baqt Treaty

The establishment of the Baqt Treaty between the African Kingdom of Makuria and the Arab Caliphate of Rashidun was a unique agreement in world history. At the time no such agreement has ever been made between a Muslim and non-Muslim nation. This type of peace treaty was unique and it allowed Muslims and Christian to coexist peacefully and trade with each other. The stipulations of the Baqt were are follow:

- Arab Muslims were not allowed to permanently settle in Nubian territory.
- Nubian Christians were not allowed to permanently settle in Rashidun territory.
- The Arab Muslims would not attack the Nubians
- The Nubians would not attack the Arabs
- Nubia would return Arab slaves who escaped to Nubia.
- Arabs would send Nubia regular packages of wheat and lentils.

The treaty established the foundation for mutual trade and prosperity between the two kingdoms. The Kingdom of Makuria would import from the Arab Muslim world luxury goods such exotic vegetables, textile good, carpets, lentils, wheat and vinegar. The Arab Muslims would import from Makuria goods such as ivory, leopard skins, dates, ebony, furniture, spears, and exotic African animals such as lions, monkeys, elephants and giraffes. Previously in 640 AD Muslims from Arabia had established control of Egypt during the expansion of the Islamic Caliphate. At times the agreement between the Arabs and the Africans of Makuria became contentious such as in 758 AD when the Arab Governor of Egypt wrote to the Kingdom of Makuria the following:

"Here no obstacle is placed between you merchants and what they want (they are) safe and contented wherever they go in our land. You however, behave otherwise, nor are our merchants safe with you".

However, such contentions were minimal and the Baqt Treaty remained in place between the two kingdoms for over 700 years. The Great Kingdom of Makuria lasted almost 1000 years until it declined in 1312 AD.

African Proverb

"Only a fool tests the depth of a river with both feet".

CHAPTER 8

Ancient Egypt

Ancient Egypt was located in north-eastern Africa along the longest river in the world named the Nile River. The early African Naqada III civilization which previously occupied the region came to an end in around 3100 BC and developed into the foundations of the what would become world famous empire of Ancient Egypt. Early Egypt had been divided into two regions namely Upper Egypt and Lower Egypt. Upper Egypt was located just north of Nubia next to the Nile River and had as its capital the city of Nekhen. Lower Egypt was located in the northern part of Africa again next to the Nile River and had as its capital the city of Memphis. Generally speaking Upper Egypt (southern Egypt) was more urbanized with cities such as Thinis and Naqada already established while Lower Egypt (northern Egypt) was more rural with a keen focus on agriculture. The pre-dynastic Egyptians of Upper Egypt were already engaged in vigorous trade with Nubia and Ethiopia and had been since around 3800 BC. Ancient Egypt was also known as 'Kemet' which means 'black land'.

The Creation of a Unified Egypt

The creation of an Ancient Egypt can be credited to the unification of Upper and Lower Egypt into a single kingdom by the African King Narmer. The wife of Narmer was the African Queen named Neithhotep which means "is satisfied". Both Upper and Lower Egypt has insignias which represented the two regions of Egypt. Lower Egypt was represented by the Egyptian Cobra and Upper Egypt was represented by the Egyptian Vulture. The double crown which represent the unification of both of these regions is known as the 'Pschent'. The ancient African artefact which is known as the Narmer Palette is piece of soft dark grey siltsone and has carved into it a depiction of King Narmer dates back to 3100 BC. The

Narmer Pallet depicts King Narmer wearing the double crown known as the 'Pschent'. King Narmer also known as 'Menes' is well known as the first official king of unified Egypt and he founded of one of the greatest African civilizations the world has ever known. It is worth noting that the extensive history of Egypt is worthy an entire book in itself.

The Narmer Palette

The palette of Narmer is also an example of early hieroglphics and is often described as the fisrt historical document in the world. The palette is over 62 cemtimeteres tall. Carved into the stone are hireoglyphics which depict Pharoah Narmer wearing the White Crown of Upper Egypt and holding a mace over another man. The Egyptian dieties, Horus, Hathor and Bat are also depicted. The symbol of Lower Egypt is also depicted. The palette tells the story of the might and power of Narmer and his success at unifying both Lower and Upper Egypt into a single kingdom.

The Rise of Egypt

After the unification of Egypt into one powerful kingdom was concluded, the 1st Dynasty of Egypt was established by King Narmer and from that time onwards the king's of Egypt became known as Pharaohs. Ancient Egypt was divided into a series of dynasties from the 1st Dynasty in 3100 BC to 31st Dynasty in 332 AD. The Historians have grouped each of Egyptian dynasties into a series of Kingdoms and Periods namely, The Early Dynastic Period, The Old Kingdom, The First Intermediate Period, The Middle Kingdom, The Second Intermediate Period, The New Kingdom, The Third Intermediate Period, The Late Period, The Macedonian Period and the Ptolemaic Period.

The Early Dynastic Period and Old Kingdom

The Early Dynastic Period is characterized as the period of time from inception of Ancient Egypt by Pharaoh Narmer in 3100 BC until the beginning of the Old Kingdom in 2686 BC and the rise of Pharaoh Djoser who established the 3rd Dynasty of Egypt. The Old Kingdom is characterized as the period of time from 2686 BC until the rise of Pharaoh Mankare in 2181 BC. In the early first 919 years of Egypt we find the implementation of a royal family, government, administration, ministers, treasury and judiciary. The Egyptian writing system known as hieroglyphics had started in 3500 BC and was used throughout the entire history of Ancient Egypt. The first pyramids where designed and constructed during this period as well. The pyramid architect known as Imhotep worked under the leadership of Pharaoh Djoser and designed for him the Pyramid of Djoser located in Saqqara.

Agriculture and Hunting in Ancient Egypt

To feed the population the Egyptians engaged in numerous forms of hunting and fishing for food. In Egyptian territory there were many animals available to hunt on land including deer, wild ass and hares. The Africans of Ancient Egypt also captured the fish from the Nile River. Other water based animals such as turtles, mussels and hippopotami were also available to be captured and eaten. In the desert region the Egyptians had a selection of additional animals to hunt including antelope, jackals and gazelles. While the meat of animals could be used for food the skins of the animals in some cases could also be sold. From the time of the Naqada who were the predecessors to the Ancient Egyptians, Africans in the region had been cultivating the local plants such as 'sorghum' in the region for food. Sorghum is a plant native to Africa which is rich in vitamin B and protein. Other sources of food such as fruits could be picked and eaten including melons and dates.

By 3000 BC farming villages had been established along the banks of the Nile and the raising of cattle such as goats and sheep had become popular which provided a consistent food source. The Egyptians were blessed with fertile land near the Nile River and benefited heavily from being able to develop canals and water systems to help grow crops such as wheat and barley and reap a generous harvest. The Egyptians utilized cows to plough the soil and they planted seeds and also used hoes to tend. In addition, the Egyptians developed vineyards for the growing of grapes and production of juices and wine. The baking of bread and cakes using honey was also very popular.

The Administration of Ancient Egypt

From the time the Egyptians established their government and administration they began to impose taxation on the populous. Taxes could be paid with goods when required and they were collected by administrators of the respective division known as a 'Nome'. In Egypt a 'Nome' was the name for an administrative division of Egypt. Egypt was divided into a total of 42 administrative divisions with 20 in Lower Egypt and 22 in Upper Egypt, all tax revenues from each division was managed by the Royal Vizer. The royal Vizier was the highest position in Egypt underneath the Pharaoh.

Mining in Ancient Egypt

The Ancient Egyptians benefited from the rich mineral deposits available in this region of Africa. Both the Egyptians and the Nubians to the south engaged in mining across their respective kingdoms. The Egyptians mined for copper and gold which was fashioned and traded. The Egyptian copper mines were located in their eastern desert. To the south in the area called Aswan quartzite, tin and lead were mined. Also, limestone and alabaster were mined and then crafted into artefacts. In the north of Egypt there were located quarries, for quartzite, alabaster and natron. From all of the sources jewellery, amulets, crowns and other artefacts were used to decorate the temples, palaces and homes of the Egyptians.

The Key Cities and Fortresses

From the time of inception, the Ancient Egyptians began to construct numerous cities and fortresses across their territory of both Upper Egypt and Lower Egypt.

Memphis: The city of Memphis was located in Lower Egypt in the north of the region just west of the Nile River. The city of Memphis was founded by the first Pharaoh of Egypt Narmer in 2925 BC after the unification of Upper and Lower Egypt. Memphis is also the location of the Temple of Ptah which was a key deity in Ancient Egypt. Memphis was the first capital of Ancient Egypt and home to many pyramids including the Pyramid of Djedefre. Pharaoh Djedefre ruled Egypt in 2575 BC.

Thebes: The city of Thebes which is also known as 'Waset' was located in Upper Egypt in the south of the region. Thebes became the religious and administrative capital of the empire by 2000 BC. Multiple annual festivals were held at Thebes and the deity Amun was prominent in the city. Over 75,000 people lived within the city at its height.

Akenhaten: The city of Akhenaten was constructed by the Pharaoh Akhenaten during the 18th Dynasty of Egypt. The city was located in Upper Egypt on the east bank of the Nile River. The city was later known as Amarna. Akhenaten and his followers were monotheists and the one God Aten was worshipped within the city and the Temple of Aten and the Tomb of Akhenaten is also located there.

Nekhen: The city of Nekhen was located in Upper Egypt in the south of the region and is also known as Hierakonpolis or the City of the Hawk. In the early stages of Ancient Egypt in 3400 BC the city of Nekhen was the religious and political capital. The city is also the location of the famous Narmer Palette which contained some of the first hieroglyphic inscriptions which depict the Pharoah Narmer and his conquest and unification of Upper and Lower Egypt.

Pyramid Architecture

The Africans of Ancient Egypt were extremely advanced in the area of architectures and construction and over a 1000-year period focused on developing a series of pyramids across their empire. The first pyramid designed and constructed by the Egyptians was the Pyramid of Djoser which is also known as the Step Pyramid. The Pyramid of Djoser was located north of the city of Memphis and was built by Pharaoh Djoser in 2650 BC. The largest of the pyramids was the Pyramid of Khufu also known as the Pyramid of Giza which is developed from 2.3 million limestone blocks which weigh 3 tons each, the pyramid stands at 146 meters in height and is 230 meters in width. The Egyptians eventually constructed over 100 pyramids in Egypt and there was a requirement to organise thousands of labourers who were overseen by the 'Overseer of All the Kings Works'. The Overseer of All the Kings Works was the name of the position given to the man who was responsible for the design, position and construction of the pyramid. One of the earliest pyramid architects was an Egyptian scientist and engineer named Imhotep who is credited with the development of the Pyramid of Djoser. Imhotep is considered a genius and polymath who also held the title of 'Director of Public Works in Upper and Lower Egypt' and 'Recorder of the Annals'. Pyramids typically were located to the west of the Nile River. As the sun also sets in the west this was considered the resting place of the dead.

Egypt and Nubia

As we mentioned before The Nubian Empire was located just south of Egypt and was established in 4800 BC. Nubia like Egypt was originally divided into Upper Nubia (southern) and Lower Nubia (northern). The early Nubians engaged in trade with the early pre-dynastic Egyptians who were known as the Naqada. After the unification of Upper and Lower Egypt and the establishment of Ancient Egypt trade continued. The Egyptians referred to Nubia as the Land of the Bow due to their expertise in warfare using the bow and arrow. Nubia was also known as Ta Seti. The relationship between the two empires was usually peaceful and they engaged in the trade of copper, ostrich feathers, pottery, exotic animals, fruits, wood, and gold. The Nubians has greater access to goods from central Africa and the Egyptians had greater access the markets of the Mediterranean and Europe due to their respective geographical locations. In 1290 Pharaoh Seti I came to power and launched military campaigns against Nubia and also Libya. In 760 BC the Nubian Empire took full control over Egypt and became the 25th Dynasty of Egypt.

The Egyptian Dynasties

Egyptians divided up the time periods of their kingdom into dynasties of which there were 31 and in addition there were periods and kingdoms that grouped these dynasties.

1. Early Dynastic Period
2. Old Kingdom
3. First Intermediate Period
4. Middle Kingdom
5. Second Intermediate Period
6. New Kingdom
7. Third Intermediate Period
8. Late Period
9. The Roman Period

The 31 Dynasties of Egypt were as follows:

The First Dynasty: Establishment Date was 3100 BC: The historians who have debated this date include Chinweizu, Rohl, Petrie, Manetho, Wilkinson, Meyer and MacNaughton. The first dynasty of Egypt was established by the first Pharaoh Narmer when he unified Lower and Upper Egypt.

The Second Dynasty: Establishment Date 2890 BC: The second dynasty of Egypt was centred in Thinis in the east of Egypt along the Nile. The first pharaoh was Bawnetcher and the last pharaoh was Khasekhemui.

The Third Dynasty: Establishment Date 2686 BC: The third dynasty of Egypt had its capital in Memphis. The first pharaoh was Nebka and the last pharaoh was Huni.

The Fourth Dynasty: Establishment Date 2613 BC: The fourth dynasty of Egypt was a peaceful period and many pyramids were built. The first pharaoh was Sneferu and the last was Thampthis.

The Fifth Dynasty: Establishment Date 2494 BC: The fifth dynasty of Egypt began with the pharaoh Userkaf and the last was Unas. The capital at this time was in Elephantine.

The Sixth Dynasty: Establishment Date 2345 BC: The sixth dynasty of Egypt began with the pharaoh Teti and the last was Nitocris.

The Seventh Dynasty: Establishment Date 2181 BC: The seventh dynasty of Egypt had a total of 4 Kings in 75 days. This was a turbulent time in Egypt's history.

The Eighth Dynasty: Establishment Date is uncertain: The historian Africanus has claimed there were 27 kings across this period.

The Ninth Dynasty: Establishment Date is 2160 BC: The ninth dynasty of Egypt was established *in* Henen-nesu which was in Lower Egypt (Northern Egypt) near the east. The name translates into "House of the Royal Child". There were 18 kings during this dynasty.

The Tenth Dynasty: Establishment Date is 2130 BC: During this dynasty the kingdom had become somewhat divided. The pharaoh's Meryhathor and Netjerikare were the first rulers however the order is disputed amongst historians.

The Eleventh Dynasty: Establishment Date is 2125 BC: The first two thirds of this dynasty are thought to have overlapped slightly with the 10th dynasty. However, they all ruled from Thebes which was in the south in Upper Egypt. The eleventh dynasty re-unified Egypt and the first Pharaoh was Mentuhotep I. The last African Pharaoh of the eleventh dynasty was Mentuhotep IV.

The Twelfth Dynasty: Establishment Date is 1991 BC: The twelfth, thirteenth, and fourteen are often grouped together and called the Middle Kingdom. The first Pharaoh of the twelfth dynasty was Amenemhet I. The pyramid of Amenemhet I was constructed in Lisht in Lower Egypt and was 55 meters in height.

The Thirteenth Dynasty: Establishment Date is 1803 BC: The founder of the thirteenth dynasty of Egypt was Khutawyre Wegaf and the capital was Itjtawy. There was a total of 60 Pharaohs during this dynasty and these Africans were attacked from invaders from Asia named the Hyksos.

The Fourteenth Dynasty: Establishment Date is 1705 BC: The first pharaoh of the fourteenth dynasty was Nehesi. Pharaoh Nehesi was from the Nubian Empire which operating alongside the Egyptian Empire at this time. The name Nehesi means "The Nubian".

The Fifteenth Dynasty: Establishment Date is 1674 BC: The rulers of the fifteenth were foreign invaders from Asia called the Hyskos who had been at war with the Egyptians for a number of years. The Hyskos Kings at this time had managed to take some of the territory of Lower Egypt (northern Egypt) and ruled from their capital in the north called Avaris. However, Upper Egypt (southern Egypt) remained under African control and they ruled from Thebes.

The Sixteenth Dynasty: Establishment Date is 1660 BC: The sixteenth dynasty saw the continued ruled of the foreign invaders called the Hyskos controlling a good portion of Egypt. Eventually the African Kings of Thebes rebelled against the Hyskos Kings. The Hyskos attempted to form an alliance with the Nubian Empire to the south against the Egyptian but this was rejected. The Hyskos eventually fell and control of Egypt came back under African control with the establishment of the seventeenth dynasty.

The Seventeenth Dynasty: Establishment Date is 1580 BC: The seventeenth dynasty was responsible for the removal of the foreign influence and control of Egypt by the foreign invaders, the Hyskos. Sekenenra Taa (translates as "the Brave") and his son Kamose were two of the African Pharaohs that conquered the Hyskos after numerous military campaigns.

The Eighteenth Dynasty: Establishment Date is 1549 BC: Ahmose I was the first pharaoh of the eighteenth dynasty. The eighteenth dynasty also include many other well know African rulers of this time including Akhenaton one of the first founders of monotheistic religion in the region (the belief in only one God). Also, Tutankhamun (King Tut), Thutmose, Nefertiti (co-founder of monotheism) and Hatshepsut (the longest female ruler of an Egypt).

Nineteenth Dynasty: Establishment Date is 1292 BC: The first pharaoh of the nineteenth dynasty was Ramesses I who was followed by Seti I and Rameses II. The nineteenth dynasty had many wars with the neighbouring Hittie Empire who were from modern day Turkey in the middle east. One of the most famous battles between these two groups was the Battle of Kadesh which the Africans won.

The Twentieth Dynasty: Establishment Date is 1189 BC: The first pharaoh of the twentieth dynasty was Setnakhte and his wife was Tiy-Merenese. A total of ten pharaohs ruled the twentieth dynasty and at this time the High Priests assisted in ruling the region of Upper Egypt. In addition, Egyptians at this time engaged in wars with Europe whom they called 'Sea Peoples' on account of their use of ships. The Africans successfully repelled the European invaders.

The Twenty-first Dynasty: Establishment Date is 1069 BC: The pharaoh Smendes was the first pharaoh of the twenty first dynasty. This period in Egypt's history is known as The Third Intermediate Period. The twenty first dynasty of Egypt ruled from the city of Tanis in Lower Egypt (northern Egypt).

The Twenty-second Dynasty: Establishment Date is 945 BC: The pharaoh Shishak I (also known as Shoshenq I) was the first pharaoh of the twenty-second dynasty. The pharaoh Shishak is mentioned in the Bible in 2 Chronicles 12:1 as attacking the Jews of Jerusalem. The Bible mentions the following:

"After Rehoboams position as king was established and he had become strong he and all Israel with him abandoned the law of God because they had been unfaithful to the God, Shishak King of Egypt attacked Jerusalem in the fifth year of King Rehoboam with twelve hundred chariots and sixty thousand horsemen and the innumerable troops of Libyans, Sukkites and Cushite's that came with him from Egypt, he captured the fortified cities of Judah and came as far as Jerusalem. Then the prophet Shemiah came to Rehobaum and to the leaders of Judah who had assembled in Jerusalem for fear of Shishak, and he said to them:

"This is what the Lord says, you have abandoned me therefore, I now abandon you to Shishak"."

Shishak is mentioned at Karnak in Egypt near Thebes at the temple of Amun, here depictions on the walls tell the story of Shishak attacking the Judah. On the right side of the image we see Shishak about to club a group of people foreign to Africa and on the left side the Egyptian deity Anum is leading off captive cities with ropes. Shishak is also known to have attacked the city of Megiddo. It is understood that Shishak's father was Meshwesh. The Meshwesh were an African tribe from Libya. Libya is located to the west of Egypt. Shishak also launched several military campaigns against the peoples of the Middle east including Syria, Lebanon and Phoenicians. Shishak was succeeded by his son Osorkon I who became the second pharaoh of the twenty-second Dynasty.

The Twenty-third Dynasty: Establishment Date is 837 BC: The first pharaoh of the twenty-third dynasty was Pedubastis and was also of Libyan descent. At this time the Egyptian Empire has two rulers simultaneously as Pedubastis ruled Upper Egypt and Shoshenq affiliated with the twenty-second Dynasty of Egypt ruled Lower Egypt. Power was split between these two African Kings with minimal conflict.

The Twenty-fourth Dynasty: Establishment Date is 732 BC: The first pharaoh of the twenty-forth Dynasty of Egypt was Pharaoh Tefnakhte and had his capital in Sais Lower Egypt. The twenty-forth Dynasty of Egypt was short compared to the previous dynasties and consisted of only two pharaohs namely Tefnakhte and then Bakenranef.

The Twenty-fifth Dynasty: Establishment Date is 785 BC: As mentioned previously by around 785 BC the Nubians to the south of Egypt had regained control over the entire Egyptian Empire and established themselves as the 25th Dynasty of Egypt. The son of the Nubian King Alara was King Kashta who led the initial conquest of Egypt and with the help of his son Piye later brought the nation under the control of the Nubians. Sometimes this period of time in Nubian history is called the Napatan Era derived the name Napata in Nubia which was the capital of Nubia at the time.

There were a number of regional rulers along the Nile in place at the time when Piye advanced and conquered Egypt. Some of these rulers included Nimlot of Hermopolis (a ruler in Lower Egypt), Aputt II (a ruler in Lower Egypt) and Osorkon IV. Using a mixture of alliances and wars the Nubian King Piye was eventually able to overcome these rulers and establish himself as the Pharaoh of Egypt.

Later the 25th Dynasty, Egypt came under attack by foreigners. The Assyrians attacked Egypt in 690 BC and later in 525 BC the Persians invaded and took over Egypt. Then the Greeks ruled Egypt from 305 BC followed by the Romans in 30 BC and finally the Arabs in 639 AD.

Egyptian Deities

The Egyptians worshipped numerous deities as part of their religion such as:

1. **Ra:** The god of the sun.
2. **Isis:** The goddess of magic

3. **Osiris:** The god of life and death
4. **Horus:** The god of the sky
5. **Sobek:** The god of the Nile River
6. **Seth:** The god of the dessert
7. **Nephthys:** The god of death and decay
8. **Geb:** The god of the earth
9. **Nut:** The god of the sky
10. **Thoth:** The god of scribes
11. **Ma'at:** The goddess of law, morality and justice
12. **Ammit:** A god of the underworld, also known as the soul eater.
13. **Anubis:** The god of the dead
14. **Bast:** The goddess of protection and cats
15. **Hathor:** The goddess of love, beauty, dancing, music and fertility

The Egyptian religious systems also contained a mythology which explained the relationships between their deities and the stories behind them. The Egyptians had numerous myths which explained the universe as they understood it at that time. Inside the Egyptian mythology we find short stories and principles.

Egyptian Hieroglyphics

The ancient Egyptians established a written language called 'hieroglyphics' which utilized symbols and images. The system of hieroglyphics was first created just prior to the development of the first dynasty of Egypt. It is known that the origin of hieroglyphics came from the Naqada culture in around 4000 BC. The latest known inscription in hieroglyphics was found at temple Philae and is dated at around 396 AD. The hieroglyphics are constrcuted in three forms, firstly the logogram which is where a symbol is representative of an entire concept. Secondly, the phonetic gyphs which are simlar to letters and function in the same way as a traditional alphabet. Thirdly a semagram or determinative which catergorize both the logographs and word made up of letters. Hieroglypics were used to describe the history, mythology and knowledge of the Egyptian people. Hieroglypics were wriitten on both temple walls, large scale monuments, stone carvings and on papyrus paper. For example the papyrus scrolls dated at around 2560 BC describes the construction of the great pyramid of Giza.

Egyptian Mathematics

The use of mathematics had been in place in Africa since 43,000 BC as depicted in southern African artifacts such as the Lebombo Bone. In early Egypt, we find evidence of mathematical artifacts at around the time of Pharoh Narmer in 3100 BC in the form of the Narmer Macehead. The Narmer Macehead is a stone artifact found in the Upper Egypt in the city of Nekhen. The macehead depicts some of the events surrounding the reign of King Narmer and also a register of the spoils of some of his wars. The macehead records that 400,000 cattle, 1,422,000 sheep and 120,000 men were appropriated by King Narmer during the unification of Upper Egypt and Lower Egypt. The Egyptians developed a base 10 numerical system. The base 10 system is in use today and is also known as the decimal system. So for example in egyptian mathemtics you can take a number such as 937 where base ten refers to the position. In 937 the number 9 is in the 1's place, the number 3 is in the ten's place and the number 7 is in the hundreds place. Each number is 10 times the value to the right of it.

The Golenishchev Mathematical Papyrus

The Golenishchev Mathematical Papyrus (paper) which is also known as the Moscow Mathematical Papyrus is an Egyptian mathematical artifact taken from Africa by the Russian explorer Vladimir Golenishchev in 1893 AD and later stored in the Puskin State Museum of Fine Arts in Moscow, Russia. This papyrus is 18 foot long and 3 inches wide contains 25 mathematical problems and their solutions. The papyrus is thought to be a product of the 12th Dynasty of Egypt and created in around 2055 BC. Examples of the mathematical problems written on the papyrus include calculating the length of a ships rudder (contraption used to the stir a boat), calculating the output of workers, calculating the area of triangles and the volume of a pyramid.

The Rhind Mathematical Papyrus

The Rhind Mathematical Papyrus is an Egyptian mathematical artifact which dates back to 1650 BC during the time of the 16th dynasty of Egypt. The papyrus manuscript is 536 centimetres in length and 32 centimeters in width. The opening writing of the manuscript states that it documents:

"the accurate reckoning for inquring into things, and the knowledge of all things, mysteries and all secrets".

The papyrus provides for its reader a selection of 20 algebraic problems, 20 arithmetic problems and also some geometric problems. The artifacts is named after the Alexander Henry Rhind who took the artifact from Egypt in 1865 AD.

The Egyptian Book of the Dead

The Egyptian Book of the Dead dates back to 1550 BC and is a collection of religious documents also known as funeral texts. This ancient African artefact provides numerous magical spells which were to be used to assist the deceased Egyptian in his or her journey to the afterlife. Magic and spells were used extensively in ancient Egyptian culture and known as Heka. In ancient Egypt Heka was used to activate the soul which was known also as 'Ka' and is divided into 5 aspects.

The 5 aspects of the soul were known as Ib (heart), Ren (name), Ba (personality), Sheut (shadow) and Ka (the vital spark), it was understood that death occurs when Ka leaves the body of an African. The Egyptian Book of the Dead contains 192 magical spells which could be used to protect the deceased African from evil forces upon his or her death. The Egyptians also believed that speech and action were similar in nature both having the ability to create. In the Egyptian belief system upon death a human would eventually be led to the deity Osiris where he or she would be judged and need to confess that they had not committed any of the 42 sins. The 42 sins that the Egyptian would need to confess that they had not committed in their life included "I have not committed robbery with violence", "I have not stolen", "I have not cured God", I have not polluted myself" and "I have not stolen cultivated land" amongst others.

The Turin Royal Canon

The Turin Royal Canon is an artefact from Egypt which dates back to their 19th Dynasty. The artefact is a papyrus which was developed around the year 1230 BC and provides for its readers a chronology of pharaohs of Egypt before the rule of Ramses II. The Royal Canon is also known as the 'Turin King List'. The papyrus contains the names of the pharaohs and also to which family group they belonged and in addition the number of years that they ruled inclusive of the months and days. To date this is one of the most detailed documents from the Egyptian Empire related to the order of the pharaohs and is divided into eleven columns. There is also some mention of the Egyptian deities.

The Egyptian Pyramids List

The ancient Egyptians constructed as did their relatives the ancient Nubians, many pyramid structures across north-eastern Africa. A total of 100 pyramids were constructed by the ancient Egyptians. Some of the most notable pyramids of Egypt included Abu Rawash in the northern part of Egypt. This pyramid was originally one of the largest pyramids built in Egypt. One of the most notable was the Giza Necropolis also known as the pyramids of Giza which these Africans aligned to the star system of Orion. The pyramids of Giza are the basis of the Orion correlation theory where the understanding of many African historians is that the three largest pyramids reflect the constellation of Orion. The constellation of Orion is a series of stars in the galaxy. The Bible also mentions Orion sometimes named Kislev the name for the ninth month of the Hebrew calendar and referenced in the biblical Book of Amos.

The Giza complex also incorporates the Great Sphinx of Giza which was a limestone statue of the Pharaoh Khafra. The Pharaoh Khafra was an African ruler of Egypt in around the year 2530 BC and member of the 4th Dynasty of Egypt. The region of Zawyat el Aryan is the location of the layer pyramid and the unfinished pyramid in an area located just between the south-west of Giza and the area known as Abusir. The pyramids here were constructed by the 3rd dynasty of Egypt during the rule of the Pharaoh Khaba. The Pharaoh Khaba ruled in around the year 2670 BC. The region known as Abu Sir houses a total on 14 Egyptian pyramids and is located a few kilometres north of Saqqara and was also a burial site for the ancient Egyptian capital city of Memphis in Lower Egypt which was founded by the Pharaoh Menes near the formation of the Egyptian Empire close to the rule of the first Pharaoh Narmer. The pyramids at Abu Sir are all step pyramids in that they constructed using flat platforms. On the west bank of the Nile we find located the Dashur complex where two of Egypt's largest pyramids are found.

Aten and Monotheism in Egypt

One of the first records of Africans practicing a monotheistic belief in one God in Egypt was during 18th Dynasty during the reign of Akhenaten in around 1351-1334 BC. Akhenaten was the 10th Pharaoh of the 18th Dynasty of Egypt and the younger son of Amenhotep III and Queen Tiye. The wife of Pharaoh Akhenaten was Queen Nefertiti. Prior to the rule of Akhenaten, the Egyptians had been worshipping numerous deities as listed previously. Akhenaten introduced the worship of the God Aten (a sun god) who first appeared in the 12th Dynasty. The religion that Akhenaten introduced was Atenism. Akhenaten raised the status of Aten to the one supreme god and it is thought that the Prophet Moses was influenced somewhat by this religion. Initially, Pharaoh Akhenaten permitted the worship of the other traditional deities but eventually declared Aten as the one true God and the only God. Aten was declared as the creator of everything in creation. The worship of other gods was then at this time outlawed. There is evidence in this within the great hymn of Aten. The great Hymn of Aten was one of the longest poems written at the time in praise in the one true god Aten. The hymn contains the sentence "O sole God beside whom there is none".

Part of the poem reads as follows:

> *"How manifold it is, what thou hast made!*
> *They are hidden from the face (of man).*
> *O sole god, like whom there is no other!*
> *Thou didst create the world according to thy desire,*
> *Whilst thou wert alone: All men, cattle, and wild beasts,*
> *Whatever is on earth, going upon (its) feet,*
> *And what is on high, flying with its wings.*
> *The countries of Syria and Nubia, the land of Egypt,*
> *Thou settest every man in his place,*
> *Thou suppliest their necessities"*

Akhenaten conducted a series of religious reforms which spanned 20 years which changed the traditional beliefs that had been in place for 1500 years. All of the established cults and deities and sacrifices to other gods were disbanded and idols were also banned. With the death of Akhenaten, all of Atenism and the monotheistic belief in one supreme creator also fell.

The Decline of Ancient Egypt

By 671 BC Egypt was still under the control of the Nubian Empire who's king at the time was the Nubian King Taharqo. The Egyptians and Nubians constructed the Sphinx of Taharqo from granite which was located at the Temple of Amun in Kawa which is in Nubia. A foreign nation in the middle-east named The Assyrians were also at this time gaining in power and military strength. The Assyrians were a Semitic people whose capital city at the time Nineveh which is located in modern-day northern Iraq. In 671 BC the Assyrians attacked Egypt and were successful in controlling a few areas of the empire. War began between The Nubian Empire and the Assyrians which lasted for seven years and eventually the Nubians relocated back into Nubia. The native Egyptians at this point regained control of Egypt and installed the 26th Dynasty of Egypt in 664 BC which traced its routes back to the 24th Dynasty of Egypt. During this period the Assyrians were dealing with a number of internal civil wars and were in a period of decline. Egypt used this opportunity to reassert its power beginning numerous construction projects and releasing itself from Assyrian influence.

One of the last great native Africans to rule over Egypt was Pharaoh Amasis who rose to power in 570 BC and ruled for 44 years until 526 BC when he transferred power to Pharaoh Psamtik III in 526 BC. A few months after Psamtik III took power he was invaded by the Persians. The Persians were a middle-eastern people from modern day Iran, who at the time had their capital in the Babylon which they had recently conquered. In 525 BC the Egyptians and the Persians went to war, but the Persian gained the support of the Greeks in Europe and were able to defeat the Egyptians. Nubia then went to war with Persia under the leadership of the Nubian King Nastasen. The Nubian Empire defeated the Persians and this halted any expansion further into Africa. However, Egypt after 3500 years had finally succumbed to foreign rule. After this Egypt continued however they now had foreign rulers and from time to time were able to regain control. In 404 BC the Egyptians manged to overthrow the Persian and take back control over the nation. In 343 BC the Persian attacked Egypt again and briefly took control only to be defeated by a Greek king named Alexander the Great in 332 BC.

African Proverb

"When the leg does not walk, the stomach does not eat ".

CHAPTER 9

The Kingdom of Ethiopia

The Kingdom of Ethiopia was located in eastern Africa and has been present as an empire since 1000 BC. Although what is known as the Kingdom of Ethiopia started in 980 BC, historians and scientists understand that it is the birth place of the human civilisation. The oldest human skeleton in the world was discovered in Herto, Ethiopia and is 160,000 years old. Ethiopia is also the longest uninterrupted nation on earth. The earliest fully formed kingdom in Ethiopia was Da'amat which was formed in 980 BC.

Ethiopia in The Bible

Ethiopia is mentioned extensively within the Bible, the Quran and the Kebra Nagast. In the Bible One of the more well known stories was the relationship between King Solomon of Israel and The Queen of Sheba. Sheba was the queen Ethiopia. King Solomon is thought to have lived in around 970 BC and engaged in a romatic relationship with The Queen of Sheba as written in **1 Kings 10:10** where it states

> *"And she (Queen of Sheba) gave the king 120 talents of gold, large quantities of spices, and precious stones. Never again were so many spices brought in as those the Queen of Sheba gave to King Solomon".*

Ethiopia is mentioned in other parts of the Bible such as the following:

2 Chronicles 14:9 *"Now Zerah the Ethiopian came out against them with army with thousands upon thousands of men 300 chariots, and he came to Mareshah".*

2 Chronicles 16:8: *"Were not the Ethiopians and the Libyans a huge army with very many chariots?".*

2 Chronicles 21:16: *"And the Lord stirred up against Jehram the anger of the Philistines and of the Arabians who are near the Ethiopians."*

Job 28:19: *"The topoz of Ethiopia cannot equal it, nor can it valued in pure gold".*

Acts 8:27: *"And he rose and went. And there was an Ethiopian, a eunuch, a court official of Candace, queen of the Ethiopians, who was in charge of all her treasure. He had come to Jerusalem to worship and was returning, seated in his chariot, and he was reading to the prophet Isaiah"*

Esther 1:1: *"Now in the days of Ahasuerus, the Ahasuerus who reigned from India to Ethiopia over 127 provinces"*

It is worth also noting that in Islamic tradition Ethiopia is known as Abyssinia or Al-Habasha.

Kingdom of Da'amat and The Land of Punt

The first kingdom in Ethiopia was known as Da'amat and was established in 980 BC. These dates reveal that the Ethiopian Kingdom of Da'mat was in operation at the same time as the Nubian Kingdom of Kush. The capital of Da'mat was Yeha which is located in northern Ethiopia and is home to the oldest structure in Ethiopia known as the temple of Yeha. The location of Yeha also provided easy access to the Red Sea and further east access to Yemen. Ethiopian tradition states that the Queen of Sheba established her palace in Ethiopia in year 950 BC and she is also known as Makeda. According to Ethiopian tradition the son of Queen Sheba rose to become Emperor Menilek I, the ruler of Ethiopia. Additional sites of interest in the kingdom of Da'amat include Matara which is located in modern day Eritrea and also Qohaito in southern Eritrea.

The Ethiopian's of the Kingdom of Da'amat would continue to rule the region of Ethiopia until their eventual decline in 400 BC. The Egyptians refered to the surrounding regions of The Kingdom of Da'amat as 'Ta

Netjer' (Land of God). It is thought that The Land of Punt was very close to the Kindgdom of Da'amat located in Ethiopia, northern Eritrea and Somalia. Trade between the Land of Punt and the Egyptian Empire has been recorded as far back as 1472 BC when Queen Hatshepsut made a voyage to the region during the reign of the 18th Dynasty in Egypt. However, there is evidence that the Pharoah Khufu of the 4th Dynasty was also in communication with the Land of Punt. Artifacts from the 4th Dynasty show Africans from The Land of Punt with one of Pharoah Khufu's sons elluding to the trade between the two nations. The products traded were gold, elephant tusks, frankincense, giraffes, cheetas, animal skins and myrrh.

Kingdom of Axum

After the decline of the kingdom of Da'amat in 400 BC numerous smaller african states ruled the area of Ethiopia until eventually the Ethiopians established the Kingdom of Aksum was established in the year 100 AD. The capital was moved from Yeha to Axum. The Kingdom of Aksum is sometimes refered to as The Aksumite Empire. The capital city of the Kingdom of Axum was located in Axum in northern Ethiopia but the nation itself covered all the regions of Ethiopia, modern–day Eritrea, also western Yemen and southern Saudi Arabia and so they controlled locations in both sides of the Red Sea. The city of Adulis was one of the ports which these Africans used for shipping and trade. By 50 AD the first king of the Aksumite Empire had been established and his name was King Zoskales appoximately 25 years before the Roman Empire was established in Europe. At this time the Kindgom of Kush to the north in Nubia was also still in operation.

Gold, Trade and Currency in Aksum

In around 270 AD the Kingdom of Aksum began to issue a new currency for the region and mint gold, silver and bronze coins in the capital of Aksum. Coins had been used previously in the region for trade for centuries however this new currency allowed for standardisation across the territory. There was significant trade between Rome and the Kingdom of Aksum at this time as indicated by excavation of Aksumite sites by historians. In addition Aksum sold their ivory to Persia, India, Arabia and China. The gold coins of the kingdom typically had the imgae of the ruling king imprinted upon at least one side of the coin. There are 20 kings imprinted on the coins beginning with the first Axumite King Zoscales.

The gold was imported from the Nubian Empire (modern-day southern Sudan) and used to mint the coins. Silver was also used for coins and as there was no silver mining in operation within the region it was imported from outside sources for minting in the capital of Aksum. The Kingdom of Axum expanded into other territories overseas such as Yemen and Southern Arabia which was initiated by King Gadarat in 183 AD and later King Azbah. Later under the leadership of King Ezana in 335 AD the Kingdom of Axum again expanded into Yemen and took control of the territory. As the Roman Empire fell into decline by 400 BC the kingdom of Aksum benefited even more trade and continued to be the dominant traders within the region.

The Language of Aksum

Back before the orginal kingdom of Da'amat the language of Ge'ez had been developed in Ethiopia. The Ge'ez language and also the script were in use from 900 BC by the Ethiopians. The language provides an alphabet and consists of a series of vowels and consonants. In the language both masculine and feminine variations of words are utilized and in addition a singular and plural suffix is used where appropriate. The Ge'ez script was the written version of the languge which evolved over time depending on the region of the kingdom it was being used and the script is written left to right. Akkele Guzay was an ancient site in the kindgom located in modern day Eritrea and provides some examples of the script being used. Another site called Matara in Eritrea also provides evidence of the Ge'ez language and home to Hawulti obelisk.

The Kings of Early Axum

There were numerous kings that ruled Ethiopia over approximately a 1000 year period and the first was King Zoskales who became king in 100 AD.

1: King Zoskales: 100 AD: King Zoskales was known to have began the expanison of Aksumite influence into South Arabia and also Yemen.

2: King Gadarat: 200 AD: King Gadarat continued to expand Aksumite influence and also formed alliances with control over Southern Arabia

3: King Azaba: 230 AD: King Azaba was known to have assisted a King of Himyar (in south Arabia) against their enemies, The Sabeans. The Sabeans were also located in the same region.

4: King Sembrouthes: 250 AD: King Sembrouthes was the first king to adopt the title "King of Aksumite Kings"

5: King Datawnas: 260 AD: King Datawnas and his son Zaqarnas are mentioned in stone inscriptions in Yemen as ruling over Arabia.

6: King Endubis: 270 AD: King Endubis was the first King to mint his own currency within the kingdom. His image was imprinted onto the gold and silver coins used in the region.

7: King Aphilas: 300 AD: King Aphilas continued the minting of currency and his image can be found on silver and gold coins wearing a head cloth.

8: King Wazeba: 310 AD: King Wazeba had the phrase "Let the people be joyful" printed on his coins.

9: King Ousanas: 320 AD: King Ousanas was ruling Ethiopia at the time when Frumentius as a boy (an Arab Christian born in Lebanon)

was enslaved and taken to Axum. He was later freed and became Saint Frumentius.

10: King Ezanas: 330 AD: King Ezana is credited with introducing and converting Ethiopia to the Christian religion.

Christianity in The Kingdom of Axum

Originally in Axum the Ethiopans were monotheistic and worshipped 'Waaq' which is the name of God in the Oromo religion which was in operation during the early stages and prior to the establishment of the kingdom. In around 330 AD the official state religion was changed to Christianity by King Ezana. However, Ethiopians had been converting to Christianity since 100 AD as referenced in the Bible in Acts 8:27 which comments on an Ethiopian reading the Bible out loud to Philip the Apostle who was a disciple of the Prophet Jesus. During the reign of King Ousanas two Syrian Christian boys named Frumentius and Aedesius were travelling on a Greco-Roman ship which was sailing to India was attcked by the Ethiopian Empire once it entered the territory as there was some tension between the two nations at the time. The two syrian boys were taken as slaves. Once King Ezana took control of Ethiopia he decided to appoint Frumentius as a bishop and used him to promote Christianity throughout the kingdom. The gold and silver coins minted during the regin of King Ezana have the Christian symbol of the cross on them.

In its early stages Christianity was only adopted by the upper classes and then slowly became the religion of the masses. The construction of Christian churches and monuments also began at this time. One of the more famous monuments was the Obelisk of Axum which is 24 metres in height and 160 tonnes in weight. By contrast Christians in Rome were at this time being persecuted, a program which began with the Roman Emperor Diocletian. It is worth mentioning that at this time there was also a section of the kingdom that were Jews. The Ethiopian Jews were known as Falasha or Beta Israel.

Islamic Migration to Ethiopia

By 610 AD the Prophet Muhammed had become well know and was establishing Islam and reciting the Quran in Arabia. The Quran means 'the recitation' and later became the holy book of Islam. The followers of Islam were called Muslims which means "one who submits to God". As the following of The Prophet Muhammed increased he came under attack in Mecca from members of his own tribe the Quraysh. The Quraysh were a powerful merchant tribe in Mecca, Arabia who were threatened by the monotheistic message of Islam. By 615 AD because of the persecution Prophet Muhammed ordered some of the Muslims to travel to Ethiopia for safety. The Kingdom of Ethiopia at the time was known as a place of justice and security. There were two migrations of Muslims to Ethoipia, the first was a group of 16 Muslims and the second was around 100 Muslims. This became the first interaction between the kingdom of Ethiopia and the religion of Islam. However it is worth noting that one of the first converts to Islam in Arabia was Bilal ibn Rabah who was an Ethiopian and was extremely close to Prophet Muhammed. Bilal was also the first 'Muezzin' (the person appointed to lead and recite the call the prayer). The tribe of Quraysh grew concerned that the Muslims were gaining allies in Africa and providing a safe haven for them. The Quraysh decided to persue the Muslims and visited the court of the King of Ethiopia and tried to convince the King that the Muslims were fugitives and should be retuned to Arabia. The leadership of Ethiopia however denied the request and protected the Muslims.

Prophet Muhammed's Letter to The King of Ethiopia

The Prophet Muhammed before his death began to send letters to all of the heads of state in the region including Emperor Heraclius of the Byzantine Empire in Balkans, The King of the Sasanian Empire in Persia, The Muqawis the ruler of Egypt and The King of Ethiopia. The letter to the King of Ethiopia read as follows:

"In the Name of Allah, the Most Beneficent, the Most Merciful.

From Muhammad the Messenger of Allah to Negus, king of Abyssinia (Ethiopia).

Peace be upon him who follows true guidance. Salutations:

I entertain Allah's praise, there is no god but He, the Sovereign, the Holy, the Source of peace, the Giver of peace, the Guardian of faith, the Preserver of safety. I bear witness that Jesus, the son of Mary, is the spirit of Allah and His Word which He cast into Mary, the virgin, the good, the pure, so that she conceived Jesus. Allah created him from His spirit and His breathing as He created Adam by His Hand. I call you to Allah Alone with no associate and to His obedience and to follow me and to believe in that which came to me, for I am the Messenger of Allah. I invite you and your men to Allah, the Glorious, the All-Mighty. I hereby bear witness that I have communicated my message and advice. I invite you to listen and accept my advice.

Peace be upon him who follows true guidance."

After Prophet Muhmammeds death in 632 AD the religion continued to grow and by 636 AD Islam had began to spread across the world under the Rashidun Caliphate and later the Umayyad Caliphate. Rashidun and was one of the earliest rulers (caliphs) of the islamic movement and Umayyad was a powerful family. Eventually via a combination of war and diplomacy Persia had started to become an Islamic state by 650 BC. By 654 AD Egypt (which had been ruled by the Byzantine Empire since 330 AD) had become an Islamic state. By 700 AD the shipping business of the Aksumite Empire declined slightly partly due to the lack of trade between the now Islamic state of Egypt. Previously the Aksumite Empire and the Byzantium Empire were both Christian nations and had therefore continued trade. In addition, Aksumite agricultural development also began to decline. Next Persian Muslims invaded south Arabia and the Ethiopian rule over southern Arabia ended. The Ethiopians then decided to abandon the coastal regions to the east and move more inland and the capital was moved from Axum. In 940 AD the African Jewish Queen Yodit from the Beta Israel tribe of Ethiopia attacked Axum and destoyed the majority of the churches and monuments.

Zagwe Dynasty

By around 1000 AD new Ethiopian dynasty had been established called the Zagwe Dynasty and they ushered in new golden age in Ethiopia's history. The Zagwe Dynasty created their capital at Roha (now named Lalibela) and ruled from this location for around 300 years with 11 Ethiopian kings. The Zagwe Dynasty continued to align with the religion of Christianity and constructed 11 very large churches all made of solid rock the capital in Roha. The Zagwe Dynasty re-established trade with Egypt via the Fatimid Empire who ruled Egypt at the time. The Fatimid Empire was Islamic and also one had an army comprised of African nubians and African berbers and also Turks at the time. Due to their expansion the territory that the Zagwe Dynasty governed was larger than their predecessors the Aksumite Empire and they controlled the northern highlands of Eritrea and from the coast of Adulis to Zelia (in modern-day Somalia).

The Ethiopian Church developed during this period and being isolated from other Christian movements had created its own attributes such as a strong emphasis on the Old Testament and the Jewish roots of Christianity. Around 1180 AD the Emperor Lalibela whose named translates to "the bees recognise his sovereignty" ruled Ethiopia. The Emperor Lalibela established numerous building programs due to a dream that he had of developing a new Jerusalem in Ethiopia. In the emperor's dream he invisioned a 'River Jordan' alongside a church called 'Golgotha' and another called 'Bethlehem'. The emperor then constructed the churches in alignment with his visio of a new Jerusalem. In the year 1209 AD the King Lalibela sent an embassy to Cairo, Egypt to a sultan there at the time, the embassy included an elephant, a zebra, a hyena and a giraffe. After a few hundered years the Zagwe Dynasty began to weaken brought about by internal disputes and fracturing.

Rise of the Solomonic Dynasty

In 1270 AD a ruler called Yekuno Amlak from the Amhara region of Ethiopia south of the Zagwe center of power arose and overthrew the last Zagwe ruler and proclaimed himself King. The dynasty which was founded by Yekuno Amlak became known as the 'Solomonic Dynasty' and traced it's leniage back to Prophet King Solomon and the Queen of Sheba. After this time the great Ethiopian written work called the "Kebra Nagast" was developed. The Kebra Nagast is written in Ge'ez and provides as account of the Solomonic line of the Emperors of Ethiopia and clear account of the lineage. In the Kebra Nagast it states that the first Emperor of Ethiopia was Menelik I who was the son of the Queen of Sheba and the Prophet King Solomon. Under the new Solomonic Dynasty Amahara became the capital. Upon Yekuno Amlak's death in 1285 his son who was named Yagbe'u Seyon took over and also had five sons. The Solomonic Dynasty would continue with a succession of kings until 1975 with the death of King Haile Selassie I.

African Proverb

"Patience is the key which solves all problems".

CHAPTER 10

The Empire of Ghana

Although afrcians have been living in West Africa for thousands of years The Emipre of Ghana was first established in 300 AD in Western Africa. The Empire of Ghana is also known as The Empire of Wagadou. The Empire of Ghana covered a much larger region than moden day Ghana, the total region incapsulated modern day Mali, southern Mauritania, and the area between the Niger and Senegal Rivers. The original inhabitants of this area were a group of Africans known as the Mande people who can be found to the present day all over west Africa. The oldest branch of the Mande people are known as Soninke who were the founders of the Empire of Ghana. The empire of Ghana gained strength over a period of hundreds of years from 300 AD to 700 AD when under the rulership of King Dinga Cisse the kingdom became completely unified and named the Ghana which means 'war chief' in the Mande language. King Dinga Cisse established the capital Kumbi Saleh in the centre of the region and from this point all the majority of the rulers of the empire would come from the bloodline of the Cisse clan.

The Empire of Ghana began the development of iron resources and produced weapons such as spears and had an army of over 200,000 soldiers. In addition to weaponary the iron working was used to develop farming tools and grow their agricultural industry. By 770 AD the kings of the Empire of Ghana had full control over the trade routes to the Sahara. Anyone who wanted to trade with the Africans in the Sahara had to pay a tax to the kings of Ghana. The kingdom also benefited from its location which was between the Senegal River and the Niger River. The empire became wealthy due to the salt and gold trade between West Africa and North Africa. The Arabs from the Middle-East typically bought gold from the African Berbers. The Berbers were Africans from the north and used camels to carry salt from north Africa to the Ghana Empire and trade it for gold. The empire would eventually have controlled both the gold and salt trade and also the trade routes. Within the kingdom of Ghana donkeys were used to transport goods.

The geographical position of the empire afforded them the privilege of being the middle men for trade throughout the region which was at that time called 'Western Sudan'. The Empire of Ghana extended their political power by bringing smaller neighbouring states such as Takrur (modern-day Senegal) under its jurisdiction. By 1000 AD the Empire of Ghana had expanded its territory even further west past the Senegal River, futher south to the Bambuk region, further east into the Niger and north up to the Berber city of Audoghast. The city of Audoghast had previously been independent but in 990 AD the Empire of Ghana captured it. The city of Audoghast is located in the south of modern day Mauritania in north western Africa. A detailed description of the city can be found in a historical book by Al-Bakri called the 'Book of Routes and Realms'. The city had been weakened due to fighting between the African berbers and the Arabs who had invaded the north of Africa at that time. This expansion ment that the Empire of Ghana now controlled a territory of 650,00 square kilometers which is about three times the size of Britain. Through these expansions Ghana became the most powerful empire in the region at that time.

Leadership Structure

The Empire of Ghana developed a hierarchical structure and government to rule the kingdom. The king or emperor of Ghana was assisted by a royal council which supervises all of the govermental activities. There were also lesser kings that were called emperors, and as the empire expanded they were required to help manage all of the international trade. In addition, prime ministers were appointed and governing responsibilites were delegated out to them. The prime miniters were further assisted by dignitaires who were in charge of the empires military, trade, palaces and foreign affairs with neighbouring kingdoms. The leaders of Ancient Ghana developed this complex structure of control because the size of the empire had expanded to such a great degree that it could no longer be managed by just a few kings. Using messengers and horses to convey orders may have worked at the founding of the nation with a smaller territory. However, once the empire was fully established instructions needed to be conveyed more quickly and with a growing land mass and populous under their control the use of emperors and prime ministers was required. Lesser governments under the ruling governments were formed to manage territory and trade further afield.

The Wealth of the Empire of Ghana

The income of the empire took on many forms but one of the ways in which wealth was generated was via a system of taxation. The government instituted two levels of taxation namely production and import/export. The production tax was applied to any citizens producing goods such as gold. Import and export taxes were paid by traders to the government for the ability to bring goods into the kingdom and also to take them out. The historian Al-Baki writes that "the King of Ghana places a tax of one dinar of gold on each donkey-load of salt that comes into his country. The king also places a tax of two gold dinars on each load of salt that goes out." In addition, taxes were placed on other goods including copper. The production tax was applied to gold as well as other goods that were produced in the empire of Ghana. Al-Bakri in his writing notes "All pieces of gold that are found in the empire belong to the emperor."

Then Al-Bakri goes further and explains why the emperors controlled the gold and regulated the price of it. He writes *"gold would become so abundant as practically lose its value"*. So it becomes clear that the empire levied taxes on the production of gold to limit the circulation of the commodity and thereby keep the value of gold very high. The gold produced in the empire was sold to other regions of Africa and also Europe. The locations of the gold mines were kept hidden and secret by the leadership and miners of the empire of Ghana. The africans of the empire of Ghana also instituted a type of trade called 'silent barter'. The traders would swap gold for salt and other goods without ever meeting face to face. For example North African Berbers would place their salt by a river for the West African Ghanians to inspect. The empire would use African drums which would be beaten to signify that start of the trade. The Ghanians would review the salt and if satisfied place gold by the salt and leave. The Berbers would then return and inspect the gold. This process would continue until both parties were satisfied with the quantity and amounts. In this way trade was conducted without each party ever meeting directly.

Religion in Ancient Ghana

From 300 AD to 800 AD the empire of Ghana followed local Sonike religions which included the belief in a creator God and a belief in spirits. They believed that the spirits could assist them in task they needed to perfom and goals they needed to accomplish and they would provide gifts and offerings to them. The empire had a network of spiriutal leaders and priests who conducted ceremonies and were well versed in magic. In addition there was a strong belief in the power of contacting their deceased ancestors making gifts and offerings to them in order to gain favour. Whenever any bad event afflicted these Africans they would make sacrifices and call on the help of the ancestors and also the spirits. There was a firm respect established in their belief system for their ancestors. There was also a belief in Animism, which is the belief that animals and plants also have a sprit which can be comminucated with. Religious object were in use at ritual ceremonies and masks were worn by dancers, also offerings of kola nuts were used. Certain locations could only be entered by the priests. When the kings died a tomb made of saj wood was constructed. They would bring the deceased king into the tomb on a bed with carpets and cushions. By the side of the king they placed ornaments, his weapons, and the vessels he used to eat and drink with. The vessels were filled with food and drink. The tomb was then buried and covered with soil until a small hill was created. Archaeological excavations in west Africa have found evidence of these ancient burials.

The Spread of Islam in the Empire of Ghana

By 800 AD the religion of Islam had spread to the Empire of Ghana through interactions between the Soninke Africans of West Africa and the Berbers African of North Africa. The Berbers were an indigenous black people of northern Africa. The Berbers whom had been in contact with Muslim Arabs mostly had converted to Islam by 700 AD. Once trade began to increase between the Berbers and the Empire of Ghana the Islamic traditions were slowly introduced. Many Berbers also lived in the capital of the empire in Koumbi Saleh and also Muslim converts from within the empire itself. We find that the historian Al Baki in his book called 'Kitab fi Masalik wal Mamalik' (The Book of Roads and Kingdoms) describes some of the interactions in his writing as follows:

"The city of Ghana [Kumbi Saleh] consists of two towns lying in a plain. One of these towns is inhabited by Muslims. It is large and possesses twelve mosques. There are imams and muezzins, and assistants as well as jurists and learned men. In the town where the king lives, and not far from the hall where he holds his court of justice, is a mosque where pray the Muslims who come on diplomatic missions."

As long as the visiting Muslims obeyed the laws of the empire and paid the taxes imposed on them to the king on time they continued to enjoy the security of the empire.

The Capital City of Koumbi Saleh

The capital of the Empire of Ghana was orginally two cities which grew to very large populations and eventually combined to one city with two sections. One side of the city was named El Ghaba which was the location of the royal palace and the wealthly members of the empire whose homes were constructed from stone. The other side of the city was the trading center and mostly populated by the muslim africans which also consisted of Berber africans from Northern Africa. This side of the capital was home to 12 mosques and was inhabited by 30,000 people. The city of the African non-Muslims was constructed using the more traditional materials found in west Africa such as hardened clay, wooden beams and thatch. They city of the African Muslims was mostly constructed of stone.

Tunka Manin

Upon the death of King Bassi who ruled from 1040 AD until 1062 AD his nephew took control over the Empire of Ghana. We read in the account of Al-Bakri the following "King Basi was the maternal uncle of Tunka Menin. It is their custom that the kingship is inherited only by the son of the king's sister, since he has no doubt that he is a son of his sister, whereas he cannot be sure that his son is really his own". Tunka Manin from the year 1062 AD ruled from his palace in Kumbi Saleh and is the king which the historian Al-Bakri mostly writes about. Al-Bakri describes Tunka Manin as wearing a 'high cap decorated with gold and wrapped in a turban of fine cotton'. He goes further and describes how the king receives his guests "the king sits in audience or to hear grievances against officials in a domed pavilion around which stand 10 horses covered with gold-embroidered materials. Behind the king stand 10 pages holding shields and swords decorated with gold, and on his right are the sons of the lesser kings of his country wearing splendid garments and their hair braided with gold. The governor of the city sits on the ground before the king and around him are ministers seated likewise. Tunka Manin is also credited with successfully defending the Empire of Ghana against the Almoravid Dynasty invasion in 1075 for a time.

Historians Description of the Empire of Ghana

As the Empire Ghana expanded and grew in power, wealth and territory it began to gain the attention of many other African kingdoms and also foreign nations. Many historians of the time wrote about the Empire of Ghana at various periods some of which are listed below:

Mahmud Kati

The west african writer from Timbuktu in the book 'Tarikh al-Fattash' tells how *"a certain King of Ghana in the 7ᵗʰ Century called Kanissa'ai possessed one thousand horses, and how each of the horses slept only on a carpet, with a silken rope for halter and had three personal attendants as if itself were a king."*

Ibrahim Al-Fazari

The Persian astronomer Ibrahim Al-Fazari refering to the Empire of Ghana as the *"Land of Gold".*

Abu Muhammed Al Hamdani

The Arab historian Abu Muhammed Al Hamdani saying *"Ghana has the richest gold mines on earth."*

Ibn Haukal

The Arab geogapher visted the empire and noted that *"the king of Ghana is the richest king on the face of the earth".*

Al Bakri

The Arab writer Al Bakri describes the Empire of Ghana in the 11ᵗʰ Century in the following way

"In the king's town, and not far from his court of justice, is a mosque where the Muslims who arrive at his court pray. The king's interpreters, the official in charge of his treasury and the majority of his ministers are Muslims. The king adorns himself wearing necklaces around his neck and bracelets on his forearms. The governor of the city sits on the ground before the king and around him are ministers seated likewise. At the door of the pavilion are dogs of excellent pedigree who hardly ever leave the place where the king is, guarding him. Around their necks they wear collars of gold and silver studded with a number of balls of the same metals.

The audience is announced by the beating of a drum which they call duba made from a long hollow log. On every donkey-load of salt when it is brought into the country their king levies one golden dinar and two dinars when it is sent out. The best gold is found in his land comes from the town of Ghiyaru, which is eighteen days' traveling distance from the king's town over a country inhabited by tribes of the Sudan whose dwellings are continuous. The king of Ghana when he calls up his army, can put 200,000 men into the field, more than 40,000 of them archers. The gold nuggets found in all the mines of his country are reserved for the king, the gold dust being left for the people. The nuggets may weigh from an ounce to a pound. It is related that the king owns a nugget as large as a big stone.

There was a King who had as his guest a Muslim who used to read the Quran and was acquainted with the Sunnah. To this man the king complained of the calamities that assailed him and his people. The Muslim guest said 'O King, if you believed in God (who is exalted) and testified that He is One, and testified as to the prophetic mission of Muhammed (God bless him and give him peace) and if you accepted all the religious laws of Islam, I would pray for your deliverance from your plight and that God's mercy would envelop all the people of your country and that your enemies and adversaries might envy you on that account.' Thus he continued to press the king until the latter accepted Islam and became a sincere Muslim.

The king ordered the idols to be broken and expelled the sorcerers from his country. He and his descendants after him as well as his nobles were sincerely attached to Islam, while the common people of his people remained polytheists."

Rebecca Green

The researcher Rebecca Green wrote *"during the middle ages when most of the people of Europe suffered disease, fear, ignorance and oppression, the Sonike people of the Empire of Ghana enjoyed a world that was rich in culture and famous as a centre of learning".*

The Kingdom of Takrur

The Kingdom Takrur was a west African nation based in modern day Senegal established in 800 BC in parallel to the empire of Ghana. The kingdom was located between the Doue River in Northern Senegal and the River Senegal. The Africans of Takrur were originally formed from the Fulani Tribe who were located in West Africa. Similar to the empire of Ghana they were gold traders who had interactions with the African Berbers of the north. At the height of power of the Empire of Ghana they were ruled over by the empire. By 1030 AD through trade interactions with Berbers and numerous Muslim missionaries the kingdom converted to Islam. In 1035 AD the King War Jabi established Islamic Sharia Law throughout the kingdom. They became allies of the newly established Almoravid Dynasty. The kingdom of Takrur became the first fully Islamic kingdom in West Africa.

Invasion of The Almoravid Dynasty

The Almoravid's were a kingdom of African Berber Muslims from the north-western Africa who had established an empire in around 1040 AD. Previously the Empire of Ghana had been on friendly terms with their Berber neighbours to the north and traded with them for hundreds of years. The Berbers had been plagued with poverty and required access to the wealth of west Africa. Over time The Almoravids developed a large army and began to expand its territory reaching as far as Southern Spain in Europe. The Almoravids were strict adherents to Islam and first set about influencing various communities in close proximity to them encouraging them to convert to Islam. Missionaries were sent out to Kingdom Takrur in West Africa who eventually converted and allied somewhat with the Almoravid Dynasty. Once the Kingdom of Takrur was allied with the Almoravids both having adopted the same religion they felt confident to launch their campaign against the Empire of Ghana.

The campaign was not completely a military effort as the empire of Ghana was a formidable force. However, by taking over some trade the Almoravids were successful in reducing the territory of the Empire of Ghana. Furthermore, there is no historical evidence for a military takeover of Ghana by the Almoravids or evidence of the destruction on the capital city. The Kingdom of Takrur benefited by becoming independent of the Empire of Ghana once again and continued to flourish during the decline of Empire of Ghana. The Almoravid Dynasty took control of the city of Audoghast (modern day Mauritania) which had been under Ghana's control for some time. However, the influence of Almoravid did not last and the empire of Ghana killed the Almoravid leader Abu Bakr in 1087 AD after which the Almoravid influence began to decline. This invasion of the Almoravids started the decline of the empire of Ghana by compromising its influence in the region and reducing the geographical territory it controlled and therefore the capacity for the empire to manage the trade in the surrounding areas.

The Decline of the Empire of Ghana

After the invasion of the Almoravid Dynasty the empire of Ghana slowly began to decline into a series of smaller states. The kingdom of Takrur were first to regain their independence from the empire of Ghana and this was followed by the area called Diara which was in the west of the empire and also fell under the influence of Takrur. Another area which broke apart from the former Empire of Ghana was the kingdom of Kaniaga, who also became an independent state. There were a number of other reasons for Ghana's decline. The kings of Ghana began to lose their trading monopoly. At the same time drought was beginning to have a long term effect on the land and its ability to sustain cattle and cultivation. In the 11th and 12th century new gold fields began to be mined at Bure (modern-day Guinea) out of the commercial reach of Ghana and new trade routes were opening up further east. Due to the growing influence of Islam in western African at this time majority of the region formerly the empire of Ghana eventually became Islamic.

A further contributor to the decline of the empire of Ghana was the rise of the African military leader called Sumanguru who was from the Soso tribe. Sumanguru became the ruler of the newly established Kingdom of Kaniaga and became a series of military campaigns against the waning power of the empire of Ghana and was eventually successful in capturing the capital city of Koumbi Saleh. Unfortunately for Sumanguru new trading centres were established in other regions such a Djenne which is modern day Mali. Sumanguru however adhered to the traditional religious and spiritual practices of his tribe the Soso. This was one of the reasons for the lack of success in Sumanguru expanding his influence and creating a nation. Eventually another neighbouring nation called the Kingdom of Kangaba who were from the Mandinka Tribe challenged his rule which eventually led to a military conflict. The ruler Sundiata went on to help establish the Empire of Mali which eventually would arise to take over as the dominant empire in the west African region. Finally, the Empire of Ghana would split into 12 separate smaller kingdoms each ruled by a separate prince. By 1200 AD the Empire of Ghana came to an end and was replaced by the growing Empire of Mali.

African Proverb

"Judge not your beauty by the number of people who look at you, but rather by the number of people who smile at you".

CHAPTER 11

The Empire of Mali

The Empire of Mali grew out of the Kingdom of Kangaba which had been established in around 750 AD. After the fall of the Empire of Ghana declined and eventually fell, this new power began to rise in western Africa and would eventually become even larger and more powerful than the Empire of Ghana ever was.

Kingdom of Kangara

The Kingdom of Kangaba was a small nation in west African which had fallen under the control of the Empire of Ghana after its expansion across western africa. The kingdom of Kangara was comprised of the Mandika people of west africa. The Africans of Kangara were producers and traders of gold. The Kingdom of Kangara was home to numerous mines from which gold was produced which was then sold in central Ghana which was the largest market and trading center for gold in western Africa. In return Kangaba received protection from The Empire of Ghana so to some degree the relationship to was mutually beneficial. Once the Empire of Ghana declined and was broken up into 12 separate kingdoms Kangara was again able to rise as an independent nation. Just prior to the official founding of the Mali Empire there were numerous kings and queens, this period of time is sometimes refered to as pre-imperial Mali. One of the early kings was King Barmandana who came to power in 1050 AD.

King Barmandana converted to Islam and made a pilgrimage to the holy city of Mecca in Arabia (in modern-day Saudi Arabia). It became the custom at the time for the leadership of these kindgoms to be Muslims and also to make the pilgrimage to Mecca. Once the military leader of the Soso tribe named Sumanguru successfully took over the remains of the empire of Ghana he took over the capital Koumbi Saleh. The Kanagara were now forced to re-establish the gold trade with the military leader Sumanguru. Unfortunately Sumanguru was known as a cruel leader, well versed in witchcraft and magic, with a very high taxation policy and a reputation for mistreating and taking Mandinka women. Eventually the Mandinka people started to revolt against Sumangara and fearing retaliation the then ruler of Kangara fled the kingdom, however his brother named Sundiata Keita whom he had previously exiled came to power in his place.

King Sundiata Keita

Sundiata Keita returned from exile to the Kangaba region and became the leader of the Mandinka tribe and after meeting with allies and friends gathered an army and engaged in a war with the oppressive ruler named Sumanguru who had taken over areas of the former empire of Ghana in West Africa. Sundiata Keita faced off against Sumanguru at the Battle of Kirina. The battle of Kirina took place in around 1235 AD in the Koulikoro Region which is in modern day Mali, Sundiata and the Mandinka tribe were victorious. King Sundiata then began the unification of Mail in 1240 AD. King Sundiata Keita moved the capital of Mali to Niani near the Niger and Sankarani River. King Sundiata Keita became a Muslim as was the custom with the elite class in west Africa at the time but also maintained the traditions, customs and some of the spiritual local practices. As a consquence it is worth noting a mixture of Islamic customs and traditional customs became common place.

The Epic of Sundiata

The Epic of Sundiata is a classic African legend in the form of a poem which details the rise of the King Sundiata and the creation of the Mali Empire. The peoples of west Africa established an oral tradition where by information, knowledge, customs, and stories were passed down through the generation by being transmitted orally. West African historians who transmitted information orally were called 'griot's'. The griot were known to have extraordinary memories and also utilized poetry and songs to transfer the information they had to their communities. During the Empire of Mali each high ranking familiy had a griot assigned to them who would offer guidance and knowledge to the familiy members. In addition, each village and town usually had a designated griot. The Epic of Sundiata once only in oral form was eventually written down and details the culture of Mali and the Mandika, the history of Sundiata Keita and his family, the surrounding African kingdoms and tribes such as the Soso, the war between Sundiata Keita and Sumanguru, and also the creation of the Mali Empire.

Expansion of the Mali Empire

After the King Sundiata won the Battle of Kirina and defeated Sumanguru numerous west African territories fell either under his control or were allied to him. Thesa lands were known as The Twelve Doors of Mali. The lands included the following; Zaghari, Tabon, Kir, Oualata, Siby, Toron, Do, Djedeba, Bambougou, Jalo, Kaniaga and the lands of the Bozo people who were located along the Niger River. King Sundiata Keita ruled the empire of Mali for 25 years and is revered as a great king in the history of the empire. The second ruler and son of the Sundiata was Uli I and took on the title of Mansa. Mansa is a Mandinka word which means king or emperor and the title was taken by the royal line of Malian rulers from this time onwards. Mansa Uli I continued the expansion of the empire with the conquest of Bambuk near the Faleme River (modern day western Mali) and also Bundu near the upper course of the Gambia River (modern day eastern Senegal). The territory of the Empire of Mali expanded further and by 1300 AD the empire was double the size of the previous Empire of Ghana. The rulers of Mali later increased the revenue and wealth of the empire by opening the copper mines of Takedda (modern day Azelik) in the east of the kingdom.

Structure of the Mali Empire

The capital of the empire of Mali remained Niani in the west of the kingdom. A class of officials to govern specific industries within the empire were established and these were made up of Malians from important families, they were known as noblemen. The noblemen would have titles such as minister of finance, minister of agriculture and minister of fishing. The structue of the empire required a complex network of rulers and ministers due to its scale. The empire was divided geographically into different provinces and the Mansa (king) delegated power to governers who oversaw each province. The courts of the empire were divided into Islamic courts and also non-islamic courts for the inhabitants of the empire.

In 1325 AD the army of Mali captured the city of Gao which was on west bank of the Niger River. The city of Gao has previously been independent of Mali and the capital of the Empire of Gao which was established in 900 BC.

The kingdom of Goa was one of the most powerful states in western Africa at the time and therefore the capture of the city was an important achievment for the Empire of Mali. The successful operation was led by the Malian military general Sagmandia. In addition to the provinces within the empire there were also vassal kingdoms. These vassal kingdoms were semi-independent kingdoms that had formed an alliance with the empire. There were up to 24 vassal kingdoms of the empire and example of which was in Djenne. Djenne was located on the Bani River about 220 miles southwest of Timbuktu. It was one of the oldest cities in west Africa, first established in 250 BC.

The Military of the Mali Empire

The size of the standing Malian army number 100,000 men of which 10,000 men were cavalrymen who used camels and horses. The size of the army made it the second largest on earth at the time after the Mongol

Empire in China. The soldiers of the army who used spears, bows and arrows and javelins. There were various classifications of higher up members of the Malian army who were generally called Farari which means 'braves'. The farari were the commanders of the army who had officers and soldiers underneath their control.

Malian Terminology

The Farima – The Farima which means 'brave man' who road on horseback.

The Farimba – The Farimba which means 'great brave man' were of royal descent. They had the power to oversea local rulers and carry out the will of the Mansa. They commanded the calvary.

The Duukanusi – The Duukanusi which means 'impressive man of the land'. They commanded the infranty force made up of slaves. They reported to the Farimba.

The Sofa – The Sofa were helpers who followed on foot and cared for the horses of their masters and provided extra weaponry and supplies.

The Arab historian Ibn Khaldun mentioned in 1400 AD the following; *"the power of Mali became mighty. All the nations of the western Sudan stood in awe of Mali, and the merchants of North African travelled to the country".*

The Economy of the Mali Empire

The Empire of Mali eventaully became one of the wealthiest empires in human history and extended to cover over 400 individual cities at the height of its power, far exceeding the wealth and territory of its predecessor the Empire of Ghana. The Empire of Mali also controlled the city of Timbuktu which was a renowned city for both trade and advanced knowledge in science and mathematics becoming one of the premier cities of learning on earth at that time. The city of Timbuktu during the time of the Empire of Mali flourished due to it becoming one of the centers of trade in western Africa. The Malians imported salt from the region called Taghaza in the north of the empire. Taghaza was so abundant in salt mines that it was known to have structures with walls and roofs constructed from salt. The price of salt once transported to the capital of Mali was known to quadruple in price.

The city of Timbuktu contained copious sweet water wells as it had close proximity to the Niger river. Shells were also a popular medium of exchange in the kingdom. The Empire of Mali also was abundant in gold so much so that it became world renowned, evidenced by the fact that Spanish maps from the year 1375 AD represented the king of Mali holding large nuggets of west African gold. Mali by this time had become much more international in trade than their predecessors the Empire of Ghana. Gold was mined at the region called Bambuk near the upper Senegal River and at that time Mali produced almost half the gold in Africa. The goldfields of Bure were also used. The currency or coinage of Mali was known as the mithqal or dinar and was equivalent to to 4.5 grams of gold. Copper was mined in the north of the empire in the region called Takkada and traded in the south of the kingdom.

Kola nuts were grown in the forests of Akan (modern day Ghana) and thousands of tons of kola nutes were traded annually and also used in religious ceremonies such as marriages and name-giving ceremonies. The malians became heavily involved in the trans-saharan trade routes and used camels to transport salt, gold, iron, meat, dairy products, books, copper, pearls, shells, cloth, animal skins, rubber, ivory, kola nuts and ivory. The Niger river became significant in facilitating trade via the use of river boats. In addition taxes were levied on all goods traded within the empire and paid to the kings and governors. The farmers of the empire were heavily engaged in agriculture and the growing of millet and cultivation of rice and sorghum. In addition fishing and the breeding of cattle were popular and the surplus was sold. The large quantity of trade also facilitated the propogation of Islam which was the dominant religion of the empire.

Over time a class of professsional Muslim traders developed within the empire and they were called the Wangara. The Morrocan geographer Al-Idrisi descrbed the towns of the Wangara in the following way:

"they have flourishing towns and famous strongholds. Its inhbitants are rich for they possess gold in abundance, and many good things are imported to them from the outermost parts of the earth".

In the east of the empire these proffessional traders were called Dyula. In around 1400 AD it was the Dyula taders who travelled into the Akan forest (modern-daya Ghana) and developed the goldfields of Akan creating a new strand to the trans-saharan trade network.

Architecture in the Mali Empire

The style of construction of the homes in the empire of Mali was unique. The development of brick homes with flat roofs became widespread. The home builders would use mud blocks and short wooden branches. Typically the homes were of a rectangular shape and were two stories tall. The first floor of the homes was used to store goods and produce for trade and consumption while the second floor was where the family resided.

The Keita Dynasty

The Keita Dynasty was the ruling group of the Mali Empire. The Ketia Dynasty were islamic and traced their lineage back to the first muezzin in islam which was an african from Ethiopia named Bilal Keita (also known as Bilal Ibn Rabah). A muezzin is the person calls the muslims in any community to prayer. Bilal Keita whose mother was an ethiopian princess was a friend of the prophet Muhammed and one of the the first people to convert to islam and also the first african to join the religion and assist in its expansion across arabia and the globe.

According to the history surrounding the founding of the empire Bilal Ibn Rabah had seven sons one of which settled in Mali and it is from this son named Latal Kalabi that the Keita trace their lineage to. It is worth noting that all the kings of the Islamic Empire of Mali took the title of Keita to show their royal lineage such as the kings Kabala Simbo Keita, Sundiata Keita and also Mansa Musa Keita I who went on to became the weathiest king to ever walk the earth. The Keita name still lasts to the present day, the President of Mali in 1960 AD was Modibo Keita.

Mali Empire King List

Historians have recorded a total of 23 kings of Mali from the time of the founder King Sundiata Keita however we know that there were several kings before the official founding of the empire during the time of the Kingdom of Kangara. The following kings or mansa's ruled Mali from around 1235 AD.

Mansa Sundiata Keita: 1235 AD

Mansa Sundiata was the founder of the Mail Empire and the famous Malian account named the Epic of Sundiata records how he conquered the ruler Sumanguru to establish the empire after the Battle of Kirina.

Mansa Uli Keita: 1255 AD

Mansa Keita was the son of Mansa Sundiata Keita and was instrumental in developing the agricultural production. Mansa Uli Keita extended the territory to the north and added the trading centres of Walata and Timbuktu. Mansa Uli travelled to Mecca in Arabia for Hajj.

Mansa Wati Keita: 1270 AD

Mansa Wait Keita was the third ruler of the empire being adopted as a child by Mansa Sundiata Keita. He passed power onto his brother Mansa Khalifa in 1274 AD.

Mansa Khalifa Keita: 1274 AD

Mansa Khalifa Keita ruled for a short period and was not a popular leader amongst his people and was known for firing arrows at his subjects unjustly. His own people decided that he needed to be removed and he was swiftly succeeded by Mansa Abubakari.

Mansa Abubakari Keita: 1275 AD

Mansa Abubakari Keita ruled from 1275 AD until 1285 AD and was the uncle of Mansa Khalifa Keita. Mansa Abubakari was instrumental in returning the management of the empire back to its former high level.

Mansa Sakura Keita: 1285 AD

Mansa Sakura Keita was the only king of Mali not to be from the royal bloodline and was actually a slave at birth. However, it was custom in western Africa for slaves to rise into higher positions over time and Sakura became a general in the army of the Empire of Mali. Mansa Sakura also conquered Goa in eastern Mali bringing it under the umbrella of the empire. Further expansion was made in neighbouring Senegal and conquered the Wolof province named Dyolof. Mansa Sakura also went to Mecca for Hajj in Arabia but was killed on his was back by armed robbers.

Mansa Gao Keita: 1300 AD

Mansa Gao Keita was directly related to Sundiata Keita's sister making him a nephew of Sundiata.

Mansa Muhammed ibn Gao Keita: 1305 AD

Mansa Muhammed ibn Gao Keita was the son of Mansa Gao Keita and ruled for five years increasing the stability of the empire.

Mansa Abubakari Keita II: 1310 AD

Mansa Abubakari Keita II (also known as Abu Bakr II) abdicated his throne to explore the ocean with an expedition consisting of 200 ships. Mansa Abubakari Keita II eventually sailed to Brazil in south America and some of the captains returned to Mali to communicate their findings. Based on the reports of his captains later Mansa Abubakari Keita II sailed to North America with a fleet of 2000 vessels reaching there before his European counterpart Christopher Columbus in 1492 AD.

Mansa Musa I Keita: 1312 AD

Mansa was the tenth and one of the most well-known kings of the Empire of Mali. Mansa Musa took the throne after Mansa Musa and was a devout Muslim who engaged in the propagation of Islam throughout the empire and its surrounding areas. Mansa Musa I was also the wealthiest king to ever rule according to historical records. Mansa Musa invited scholars from around the Muslim world to Mali and also constructed palaces and mosques in Gao, Niani and Timbuktu. Under Mansa's leadership the Empire of Mali became one of the most powerful empires in the world at that time.

Mansa Maghan Keita I: 1337 AD

Mansa Maghan was one of Musa I's younger sons and inherited the throne from him ahead of his older brother. The wealth of the empire continued to expand under his reign and he ruled Mali for four years in total before passing on the leadership to his older brother Suleyman Keita. Mansa Maghan also had a number of sons who would rule after him.

Mansa Suleyman Keita: 1341 AD

Mansa Suleyman is credited with having a relatively long reign of 24 years after inheriting the throne from his younger brother Maghan.

Mansa Suleyman had to fend of attacks from the neighbouring Fula tribes and did so successfully. During this time the north African Berber historian named Ibn Battuta visited Mali and wrote his account in the manuscript called 'Travels in Asia and Africa'.

Mansa Keita: 1360 AD

The son of Mansa Suleyman was ruled for less than one year and was defeated by his rival Mari Djata in an internal battle.

Mansa Mari Djata Keita II: 1360 AD

Mansa Amri Djata was known for cultivating a relationship with the court of Morocco in Northern Africa sending them a giraffe and also with the north-east African court of Egypt. Mari Djata was also known for his extravagant spending.

Mansa Musa Keita II: 1374 AD

Mansa Musa rose to power and focussed his energies on redressing some of the spending of his predecessor.

Mansa Maghan Keita II: 1387 AD

Mansa Maghan was another son of Maghan Keita II reigned for two years before being succeeded by Sandaki.

Mansa Sandaki Keita: 1389 AD and **Mansa Maghan Keita III:** 1390 AD

Mansa Sandaki was a relative of Mansa Mari Djata Keita and ruled for 1 year. Mansa Maghan engaged in battles with a neighbouring tribe called the Yatenga.

Mansa Musa Keita III: 1404 AD

Mansa Musa Keita III was able to expand the territory of the Mali Empire further into the region called Dioma. Mansa Musa Keita III would pass the leadership to his brother Uli II.

Mansa Uli Keita II: 1460 AD

Mansa Uli Keita engaged in battles with the neighbouring Fula tribe and in addition the Portuguese from Europe under the command of the navigator Diogo Gomes who had attempted to invade western Africa by sea to access the natural resources of the region. The Portuguese were defeated by the Empire of Mali and returned to Portugal.

Mansa Mahmud Keita II: 1480 AD

Mansa Mahmud was the ruler of Mali as the empire began to decline and had to engage in war with numerous foreign and domestic powers. At this time the African kingdom of Songhai had also began to rise to power and took control over the salt mines of Taghaza. The empire was also engaged in ongoing battles with the Portuguese from Europe and also the African tribe the Yatenga again attacked Mali. In addition, the Fula tribes conducted various raids against the empire.

Mansa Mahmud Keita III: 1496 AD

Mansa Mahmud had the misfortune of having to rule over a declining empire at that time. The main rivals to the Empire of Mali in the west African region was the Songhai Empire. The leader of the Songhai Empire at this time was Askia Muhammed I who waged war with the Empire of Mali eventually taking control of some of its former territory. In addition, another African nation called the Empire of Great Fulo which was located just north west of Mali was also rising to prominence and by 1490 has established its first king who battled with both the empires of Mali and Songhai. At this time the empire began to lose more and more territory to neighbouring African states. Mansa Mahmud moved his residences further north due to the ongoing conflicts.

Mansa Mahmud Keita IV: 1590 AD

Mansa Mahmud became final ruler of the Empire of Mali and ended his rule in 1610. After his death his sons fought amongst themselves to divided up the massively reduced of the now remaining kingdom eventually dividing the kingdom into three distinct areas Hamana, Kangaba and Joma.

The Account of ibn Battuta

Ibn Battuta was a north African Berber Muslim historian born in 1304 AD who travelled various places including Somalia, Tanzania, South Asia, China and also the Empire of Mali. Ibn Battua wrote about the places he observed and peoples he met during his travels. In his book 'Travels in Asia and Africa' Ibn Battuta provides an eye witness account of the what he observed in The Empire of Mali in the year 1341 AD. Ibn Battuta wrote the following:

"I travelled with travel companions whose leader was Abu Muhammed Yandakan Al-Massufi, may God have mercy on him. In the company was a group of merchants of Sidjilmessa and others. We arrived after 25 days at Taghaza. Amongst its curiosities are the fact that the construction of its houses and its mosques is of rock salt with camel skin roofing. In it is a salt mine. It is dug out of the ground and is found here in huge slabs. A camel can carry two slabs of salt. The Malians arrive from their country and carry away the salt. A camel load of it is sold in Walata for eight to ten mithqals and in the town of Niani for twenty to thirty mithquals perhaps the price reaches up to forty. The Malians exchange the salt as money as one would exchange gold and silver. They cut it up and trade with it in pieces"

Ibn Battuta also had the good fortune to witnesses some of the celebrations within the Empire of Mali and also of these observations the following:

"The Mansa holds sessions during the days associated with the two festivals after the asr (later afternoon) prayers on the platform. The men at arms come with wonderful weaponry, quivers of silver and gold, swords covered with gold, their sheaths of the same, spears of silver and gold and wands of crystal. Four of the amirs stand behind him to drive off flies, with ornaments of silver in their hands which look like riding stirrups. The farariyya (commanders), the qadi (judge), and the preacher sit according to custom, the interpreter Dugha brings in his (the Mansa's) four wives and his concubines, who are about a hundred in number. On them are fine clothes and on their heads they have bands of silver and gold with silver and gold apples as pendants. A chair is set there for Dugha to sit on and he beats an instrument which is made of reeds with tiny calabashes below it, praising the sultan, recalling in his song his expeditions and deeds.

The wives and the concubines sing with him and they play with bows. There are with them about thirty of the Mansa's pages wearing red woollen robes and white caps on their heads. Each one of them has a drum tied to him and he beats it. Then come his young men who play and turn in the air as they do in India. They have a wonderful graceful and lightness in this. They juggle with swords beautifully and Dugha performs a marvellous game with a sword. At that point, the sultan orders that a gift be given him, they bring him a purse of two hundred mithqals of gold dust. An announcement of its contents is made to him over he heads of the people. The farariyya (commanders) get up and twang their bows, thanking the sultan. On the following day every one of them makes a gift to Dugha according to his means."

Ibn Battuta continues with a description of a specific incident concerning Mansa Suleyman.

"It came about that in the days of my stay in Mali that Mansa Suleiman was angry with his senior wife, the daughter of his paternal uncle, who was called Qasa which signifies the queen among them. The queen is his partner in the kinship, following the custom of the Malians. Her name is mentioned with his in the pulpit."

Ibn Battuta also describes the temperament of the Africans of The Empire of Mali

"The Malians are seldom unjust, and have a greater abhorrence of injustice than any other people. Their sultan shows no mercy to anyone who is guilty of the least act of it. There is complete security in their county. Neither traveller nor inhabitant in it has anything to fear from robbers or men of violence."

The account of Ibn Fadl Al-Umari on Mansa Abubakri II and his travels to the Americas

Ibn Fadl Al-Umari was an Arab scholar who was born in Damascus, Syria and provides an account of the Empire of Mali and in particular Mansa Abubakari (also known as Abu Bakr II) who was the predecessor of Mansa Musa. In his book called Masalik ab Absar fi Mamalik al Amsar and published in Cairo, Egypt in 1342 AD he describes historical account of the Empire of Mali's expedition to the America's under the leadership of Mansa Abubakri who came to power in 1310 AD. According to the historical record of the Empire of Mali the king Mansa Abubakari wanted to travel to the edge of the Atlantic Ocean.

The king launched 200 ships filled with men and another 200 ships stocked with enough food, water and gold to last two years and sent them out to explore. After some time one of the captain's returned in his ship and explained to the king the following details:

"King, we sailed for a long time and we encountered in mid-ocean something like a river with a violent current. The other ships sailed on and they did not come back. As for me, I returned to where I was and did not enter the current".

Mansa Abubakari decided that he would embark on a voyage himself. He prepared 1000 ships filled with men and 1000 ships filled with provisions and set sail for the Americas and did not return. It is understood that the Malians ended up landing initially in South America near the coast of Brazil in the place known today as Recife, its other name is Purnanbuco, which we believe is an aberration of the Mande name for the gold fields that accounted for much of the wealth of the Mali Empire and then travelled up into Mexico and finally North America. Mansa Abubakari's successor was Mansa Musa who took control of the empire in his absence.

The Malian voyage to the Americas in 1312 AD took place about 180 years before the Spanish explorer Christopher Columbus travelled there in 1492 AD. When Christopher Columbus and the African sailor Pedro Alonso Nino finally arrived in the America's they found evidence of Africans already present in the Americas. Christopher Columbus wrote in his 'Journal of the Second Voyage' that when he reached Haiti the Native Americans told him that black Africans people had already come from the southeast in boats trading in gold tipped spears. In 1974, the skeletons of two African males were discovered in Hull Bay in the St Thomas, Virgin Islands of the Caribbean and sent to the Smithsonian Institution of Washington D.C. for analysis. The African skeletons were dated to be between 950 AD and 1350 AD.

The analysis of the African skeletons were written up by the Douglas H. Ubelaker and J. Lawrence Angel of the Smithsonian Institution and they noted the following:

"Skeleton A represents the relatively complete, well preserved skeleton of a 33-41-year-old African adult male, approximately 170cm (67 inches) in statue. A diagnosis of male is based on the general ruggedness of the skeleton, larger mastoid processes on the skull, and the morphology of the pelvis.

Skeleton B represents an African male, between 30 and 38 years old with a living stature of about 173 cm (5 feet, 8 inches). Morphically, this skeleton is remarkably similar to skeleton A. All of the African traits documented for skeleton A are also found with skeleton B. On this basis an African, not Indian, racial origin is suggested...."

Christopher Columbus himself also made mention of the fact that he purchased metal goods from the Native Americans that were of West African manufacture. In addition, chemical analysis of the gold tips that the Spanish found on the spears indicate that they likely came from west Africa. Also, analysis of old maps of Mexico some of which were developed by the Spanish showed that the Malians named places after themselves such as Mandinga Bay, Mandinga Port and Sierre de Mali.

Islam in the Empire of Mali

The first convert to Islam in the Empire of Mali was the founder Sundiata who practiced a loose form of Islam often combining Islamic and indigenous western African beliefs. This was also the case for the majority of the population at the time. The first Malian king to make a pilgrimage to the holy city of Mecca was Mansa Uli the second king of Mali. From this period onwards the popularity of Islam spread from the leadership down to the general populous. In addition, the religion eased trade between of neighbouring Islamic kingdoms in Africa. When the Malian king Mansa Musa rose to power in 1312 AD he further established Islam throughout the empire as he was an extremely devout Muslim and used his immense wealth for the propagation of Islam. Under the leadership of Mansa Musa, the empire established ambassadors across Northern Africa and the capital of Mali Niani was then visited by Islamic scholars from those regions. When Mansa Musa returned from his pilgrimage to Mecca he brought back with him many learned Islamic scholars from other regions of Africa and established them in Timbuktu. New mosques in Gao and Timbuktu were constructed as well as new courts of Islamic law.

King Mansa Musa

The tenth king of Mali was Mansa Musa and he came to power in 1312 AD, he is also known as The Lion of Mali. After Mansa Abubakari II departed for his voyage to the Americas Mansa Musa took his place as the ruler of the Empire of Mali. Mansa Musa was an extremely devout Muslim and embarked on a large program of construction within the empire building universities and mosques in the cities Gao and Timbuktu. Mansa Musa constructed the ancient centres of learning namely Sankore Madrasah and Dijinguereber Mosque in Timbuktu. In addition, he built The Hall of Audience in the Malian capital city of Niani where some of the finest examples of architectural expertise at the time were on display and these included window frames of gold and silver, cut stone, wooden floors framed in silver foil and adornments of arabesques (geometric patterns).

Mansa Musa became famous throughout the world for his large wealth and his pilgrimage to the city of Mecca in 1325 AD. Several eyewitness accounts at the time attest to vast array of wealth that he carried with him and it is understood that he gave away so much gold away to the poor during his journey that the sudden influx of so much gold devastated the gold markets of Egypt, Medina and Mecca for the next decade. This was the only time one man had controlled the price of gold across the Mediterranean.

The historian Dr DeGraft Johnson provides the following account of Mansa Musa:

"It was 1324 AD that the world awoke to the splendour and grandeur of Mali. There across the African desert, and making its way to Mecca, was a caravan of a size which had never before been seen, a caravan consisting of 60,000 men. They were Mansa Musa's men, and Mansa Musa was with them. He was not going to war: he was merely going to worship at Mecca. The huge caravan included a personal retinue of 12,000 slaves, all dressed in brocade and Persian silk. Mansa Musa himself rode on horseback, and directly preceding him were 500 slaves, each carrying a staff of gold weighing about six pounds (500 mitkal). Then came Mansa Musa's baggage-train of eighty camels, each carrying 300 pounds (three kantar) weight of gold dust. This imposing caravan made its way from Niani on the Upper Niger to Walata, then to Tuat, and then on to Cairo. Mansa Musa's piety and open-handed generosity, the fine clothes and good behaviour of his followers, all quickly made a good impression. One might have thought that a pilgrimage to Mecca undertaken with such pomp and ceremony would have ulterior political motive, but no such motives have ever been adduced."

The Ancient City of Timbuktu

Under the leadership of Mansa Musa, the city of Timbuktu rose to become one of the premier centres for knowledge and trade in the whole of the continent of Africa and indeed the world at that time. The city also became a well-known centre for Islamic learning and was the location of the University of Sankore Mosque where scholars and students came to learn the Quran and Islamic theology as well as mathematics, medicine, law and astronomy. Mansa Musa also constructed one of his royal palaces in the city. Timbuktu became a place where many of the premier Islamic scholars from Bagdad in Iraq, Cairo in Egypt and Persia came to learn and to teach, it was home to several hundred thousand manuscripts. The king Mansa Musa constructed the three great mosques and madrasa of Mali named Sidi Yahya, Djinguereber Mosque and Sankore Madrasah all of which combine to formulate the University of Timbuktu which still operational to present day.

By 1400 AD the Sankore Madrasah had one of the largest collections of books in Africa with over 700,000 books in its collection. Although all forms of goods and services were traded within the city some of the most popular was gold, salt and books. The historian Leo Africanus reported the following regarding *Timbuktu:*

"In Timbuktu there are many judges, professors and holy men, all being generously helped by the king who holds scholars in much honour. More profit is made from selling books in Timbuktu than from any other branch of trade".

Much of the learning in Timbuktu took place within the homes of the scholars and passed to students through a chain of teachers known as 'silsila' which means link or chain in the Sufi tradition of Islam which was popular in west African.

The Sufi tradition is well known as the mystical dimension of Islam. The students would listen and learn from the sisila and write down the knowledge and study it.

By 1450 AD the population of the city of Timbuktu had swelled to over 100,000 inhabitants with over 25,000 scholars. Once the Empire of Mali declined next great empire of west Africa called The Songhai Empire took control.

The Decline of Mali

A combination of weak and ineffective rulers and increasingly aggressive raids by Mossi neighbours and Tuareg Berbers gradually reduced the power of Mali. In the east, Gao began its ascendancy while remaining part of the Mali Empire.

African Proverb

"Love is shown by deeds not words"

CHAPTER 12

Historical Timelines

The ancient empires of Africa dates back thousands of years and developed at different times in various locations across the vast continent. Below we look at a recap of each of the empires we have looked at in African Empires Book 1.

1. Early Egypt

The Halfan Culture:

    Empire Establishment Date: 18,000 BC

The Qadan Culture:

    Empire Establishment Date: 13,000 BC

2. Pre Dynastic Lower Egypt

The Faiyum Culture:

    Empire Establishment Date: 8,000 BC

The Merimde Culture:

    Empire Establishment Date: 4800 BC

The Maadi Culture:

    Empire Establishment Date: 3900 BC

3. Pre Dynastic Upper Egypt

The Tasian Culture:

Empire Establishment Date: 4500 BC

The Badarian Culture:

Empire Establishment Date: 4400 BC

4. Pre-Dynastic Egypt

Naqada I

Empire Establishment Date: 4000 BC

Naqada II

Empire Establishment Date: 3500 BC

Naqada III

Empire Establishment Date: 3200 BC

5. The Nubian Empire:

Empire Establishment Date: 4800 BC

6. Ancient Egypt:

Empire Establishment Date: 3100 BC

7. The Kingdom of Ethiopia:

Empire Establishment Date: 1000 BC

8. The Empire of Ghana:

Empire Establishment Date: 300 AD

8. The Empire of Mali:

Empire Establishment Date: 750 AD

African Proverb

"It takes a village to raise a child".

CHAPTER 13

Conclusion

So, dear reader within African Empires Volume 1 we have discovered some of the rich and long history of the African continent and we have also looked at some specific empires and kingdoms in both eastern and western Africa. We have understood that human life on planet earth started in Africa and that Africans have been present on the continent since at least 250,000 BC. We have seen how Africans were therefore the first to develop science, mathematics, agriculture and astronomy.

Then we looked at the Bantu expansion of 500 different African ethnic groups around the continent of Africa. Interestingly, we have seen that all of the major holy books of the monethiestic religions of Judaism, Christianity and Islam all mention African and African royalty specifically within their scriptures and we have seen that many of the major prophets including Moses, Solomon and Muhammed all have relationships and assistance from Africa. The hundreds of archaeological sites spread across Africa has fully illustrated the fact that many ethnic groups, nations, kingdoms and empires developed sophisticated cultures, architecture and art. We have seen the military expertise of nations such as the Nubian Empire and the Mali Empire.

It is simply astounding the contributions that Africa has made to world civilization and it is now certain that Africa is the foundation of human civilization on planet earth. Far from being one culture, we can see that multiple cultures, all African, combined to produce a rich contribution to the planet. I hope that his book has been an enlightening look at the history of Africa and an encouragement to research even more into the amazing historical record of Africa. In African Empires Volume 2 we will take a deeper look into the history of Africa expand into many other kingdoms and empires. In African Empires Volume 3 we will focus specifically on the mighty kings, queens and leaders of ancient Africa and their impact on the continent.

We look forward to meeting with you again in future publications as we journey into the incredible and fascinating historical history of the African Empires.

African Proverb

"However long the night, the dawn will break".

BIBLIOGRAPHY

The Kongo Kingdom, The Rosen Publishing Group Inc. (1998)

City-States of the Swahili Coast, The Rosen Publishing Group Inc. (1998)

The Zulu Kingdom, The Rosen Publishing Group Inc. (1998)

Great Zimbabwe, The Rosen Publishing Group Inc. (1998)

Mali: Land of Gold & Glory, Five Ponds Press (2002)

The Lost Kingdoms of Africa, Bantam Press (2012)

Timbuktu: The Sahara's Fabled City of Gold (2007)

Ancient Egypt, Oxford University Press (1997)

Ta'rikh al Fattash: The Timbuktu Chronicles 1493-1599, Africa World Press (2011)

History of Africa, Macmillan Publishers Limited (2005)

A History of West Africa 1000-1800, Longman Group Limited (1977)

Precolonial Black Africa, Lawrence Hill Books (1987)

The Adventures of ibn Battuta, University of California Press (1989)

The Almohads: Rise of an Islamic Empire (2013)

History of West Africa, The Diagram Group (2003)

The Lost World of Nubia, Infobase Learning (2012)

The Kingdom of Benin, The Rosen Publishing Group (2014)

The Ancient Kushite's, Scholastic, Library Binding (2005)

100 Great African Kings and Queens, Real African Publishers (2012)

Ancient West African Kingdoms, Heinemann Library (2009)

Ancient West African Kingdoms: Ghana, Mali, Songhai (Reed Educational & Professional Publishing)

The Kingdoms of Africa: Kanem-Borno: 1000 Years of Splendor, Chelsea House Publishers (1995)

The Kingdoms of Africa: Ancient Ghana: The Land of Gold, Chelsea House Publishers (1995)

The Kebra Nagast, St. Martins Press (1997)

The Penguin Atlas of African History, Penguin Books (1995)

Illuminating The Darkness, Ta-Ha Publishers Ltd (2012)